Julian teaches
YOU ARE UNIQUE
through June K. Burke

BURKE-SROUR PUBLICATIONS

Totowa, New Jersey 07512

Burke-Srour Publications, Inc.
20 Mountainwood Court
Totowa, NJ 07512

Cover adaptation from original design by Phillip Eric Sobel

DEDICATION

This book is dedicated to Joy and Saul Srour, who are always there and who prove beyond doubt the meaning of the word friendship.

Thank you, my friends!

June

JULIAN PUBLICATIONS AVAILABLE

Books:

Self Discovery and Manifestation
Creation, Its Laws, and You
You are Unique

The Learning Tree Booklet Series

Introduction to Meditation
Reincarnation
Problem Solving
Decade of the Nineties
Spiritual Growth

NOTE: If you are unable to obtain the Learning
Tree Series booklets at your local book store, please
contact:

Burke-Srour Publications,
20 Mountainwood Court
Totowa, NJ 07512

ACKNOWLEDGEMENTS

Giving birth to a book is not much different from giving birth to a child. The initial excitement carries you through the first phase and your pride in the product through the next. This euphoria permits you to blind yourself to the warts. You need others who care enough to check out the warts, dole out the balm, and hold your hand. I acknowledge gratefully my wart seekers and hand holders:

> My husband Bill who is my rock.
> Our children, Janet, Ellen, and Bill, who are so creative and unique themselves.
> Our granddaughter Kari Ellen, who is a wise and delightful young lady.

Next is that wonderful extended spiritual family: The New York Circle—Joy and Saul Srour, Renate Collins, Judith Lackamp, Barry and Leela Burkan, Dorothy and Frank DeSoto, George Ruby, Nicholas Theo, Blanche Duffy, and John Svirsky. Adele Lederman, Jerry Gross, Paula Hilbert, Claire Cramer, and Eleanor Johnson complete the circle.

Special thanks go to Daniel Kitchen for his hours of editing and Mark Love for his kind and helpful suggestions.

These wonderful people create a strong supportive energy. They are the greatest.

EDITOR'S COMMENTS

YOU ARE UNIQUE is the second book of Julian material that I have had the opportunity to assist in preparing for publication. My association with Julian is now some ten years old and my work with this material continues to be a powerful transforming experience.

YOU ARE UNIQUE resulted from a series of public lectures and focuses on the qualities which make each of us unique. It is our uniqueness that gives us something special to share with all those around us. The simplicity and directness of its message signify what is often lost in most teachings, that the path does not have to be complicated to be effective and that the key to self-unfoldment is an inner search that each of us must undertake and cannot be laid upon us from some outside source.

Many of the themes in this book are now quite popular in our culture. They include issues of self-esteem and relationships with others. The true validity of any teaching is its direct application to every day life, and I have found this material to be most helpful in that regard. The changes and transformation which I have experienced in using these tools lead me to an ever greater appreciation that the universe is watched over by a most loving and caring God.

It is difficult to find words that express the pleasure which has come from having been associated with the production of this book. May you also enjoy and be assisted by it.

Dan Kitchen

HOW JUNE AND JULIAN BEGAN

My association with Julian took a long time to build. It was forming even before I was totally aware of his presence. As a child, I was psychic. I knew who was on the telephone before it was answered. I knew when packages were going to arrive before the mail was delivered. I thought everybody did. Somewhere along the way, probably because of peer pressure, I ceased to use my ability. It was not intentional, it just happened.

Some twenty-six years later, I would again remember the gift. It was when my third child was born that my awareness was put in motion again. Six hours after delivering a beautiful son, I had a postpartum hemorrhage and had the death experience.

How does one describe dying? I would have to describe it as the most beautiful experience I have had in this lifetime. I experienced tunneling into light and witnessed color spectra beyond those we understand. I became aware of white light and a voice. When asked if I wished to fulfill my destiny, I agreed. I had not the faintest idea what that meant at the time. What could it possibly mean but the chance to raise my son? I was then turned around, no longer able to look into that world. Now I found myself looking down into the hospital room, watching the two teams of doctors and nurses working on me. I knew it was me, but felt no emotional attachment at all.

As I watched, I became aware of the compassion on the faces of those working on me; and the thought came that I had to go back and tell them it was okay, that I did not hurt anymore.

With the thought came the return to the body, surgery, and recovery. Now the search began.

God had always been a presence in my life, but now I wanted a more intimate realization of the God within. I wanted to know more about the world I had seen. I now remembered that psychic side of myself and wished to understand it more fully. The quest began. The path led to meditation, and the meditation to the development of deep trance work. During meditation I was prepared physically and emotionally for a safe and smooth merger of the energies that would permit us to work as a team.

J. K. B.

JULIAN'S STATEMENT

I am a Seraph of the order of Seraphim, that which you call angelic force. From the beginning of time, I have been a bridge between two worlds. I have never incarnated in a physical body.

In our varying energy patterns, angelic forces are given assignments which they carry forth in the universe. My assignment has been to be a teacher of truth, a deliverer of God's messages, and a deliverer of mankind through his own potential. Thus, from the beginning of time, I have been a bridge between the unseen world and the seen. I have watched cultures be born, come to fruition, and die. It is my job to try to know and understand the culture and the vernacular of that culture in order to help man to better his potential.

The angelic forces of the universe were created to be the friends and guardians of mankind and all creation. We have no desire other than to assist. Our fulfillment is in observing mankind's growth and transition into higher planes. Each angelic force has its own particular assignment. Some deal with the plant and nature world, others with the animal kingdom. There is no thing of God's creation in the Earth that does not have a guardian force that is overseeing its advancement within its own species.

If in speaking with you I can assist you to ponder, make decisions, and grow, it will be as it is meant to be. I am with you every step of the way.
So be it.

Julian

<u>PLEASE NOTE</u>

The use of the word "man" in these teachings refers to mankind versus the animal, plant, or mineral kingdoms. It has no reference to gender.

Julian has a way of mixing his pronouns, disregarding singular and plural; masculine and feminine; and first, second, and third person. The end result is a strong paragraph, the meaning of which is perfectly clear. Since this is typically his way of speaking, we have chosen to leave his pronouns as they are.

TABLE OF CONTENTS

The tools of a trip are a road map and a destination. The tools of life are no different.

YOU ARE UNIQUE

CHAPTER I

YOU ARE UNIQUE

Every soul is unique unto itself. It is surrounded by an energy package that becomes shaped and molded by environment and associations into a personality. Reality is that which is within. There are times when you must sift through those personality aspects of yourself to be in touch with your own reality. You will come to realize that there are sometimes conflicts within that make you feel that you do not really understand yourself. Deep within you is the reality of yourself. It is what has brought you to the Earth plane; it is what makes you different from every other person. It is the essence of your strength; it is your light and your guidance.

How do you discover your own uniqueness? How do you know when you are truly on your own path and not someone else's? How do you truly know when to accept that which you are doing as right for you? These are some of the issues we are going to focus on in this book.

Are you reacting to something because you think you are supposed to, or because you really feel it? That is one of the first questions you must ask yourself, for you should never respond to something by the dictation and direction of another unless you truly feel it inside yourself. I have a perfect example of this. There is in your world today what is called the "computer industry." One hears that computers are the way to go, that computers are it. There is some truth to this. Computers are a great and important part of the future in this particular society and culture. That is not, however, a basis on which to make this your career choice. If you are intrigued by the programming systems and the knowledge needed, then it is right for you, and you may make this your career. You do not make computers your career unless you truly feel comfortable working with this type of technology. Your own uniqueness might find you dealing with computers in quite a different manner. Perhaps your own uniqueness says, "Go sell them, but don't use them. I know enough about them to sell them, and selling is my thing." Then computers can still comfortably be a part of your life.

Most people have felt uncomfortable at some time about something they are doing. I am not talking about being guilty because they are doing something they know is morally wrong, but that feeling that they somehow just don't fit the mold.

Before you enter this Earth plane, you decide a great many things about yourself—areas of soul growth, areas of karmic debt, and things you would like to accomplish. You await the configuration of the heavens that will give you the energy package that will make you able to encounter and encompass those soul growth areas. Thus, each person through their unique energy is evolving mentally, physically, and spiritually. The vehicle for this growth is your own special uniqueness, your own energy. When two people do not see eye-to-eye, it simply means that they are approaching something through a different energy. In the realization and acceptance of that, there need not be friction. There can be acceptance that it is all right to see things from a different perspective.

Your uniqueness demands to be known in many ways. There are the seven-year cycles of aggression that everyone goes through. Every seven years, the inner you demands to be known as an individual, separate from the collective. When you look back at the ages of seven, and fourteen, and twenty-one, you may recall that at those periods in time, there was a sense of the back straightening up, the heels digging in, and the chin coming up, all saying, "I'm me. I'm not going to be swallowed by society, or anyone else; I'm going to be me." Whether you actually do anything about it or not is entirely your own decision. The feeling is there, a feeling of uneasiness—what you might call "antsy." It is a sense of the need for movement without knowing where the movement is going. It is a sense of feeling stagnant. These feelings are urges pushing you to move forward into a new aspect of yourself.

As a unique individual, you function within a confined space. You are within the laws and the imperatives designed and created by the culture. They, in turn, fall under Universal Law. Uniqueness does not mean oddness or blatant showmanship. Many people think it is unique to be bizarre, and that is not the object. Uniqueness says, "I know

who I am, and I am going to use my full potential and let
that become a living part of my universe." That does not
mean that you cannot enjoy the bizarre, but see that as part
of the personality. Under all that is the true impetus that is
pushing you to your success—the desire to be *you*, no one
else.

Recognize that there are both the written laws of the
land, and those unwritten laws that society forms. Society
says one doesn't go to a formal dance in a bathing suit!
Your uniqueness lets you function *within* those laws without feeling undo pressure. If you do not like the law, then
use *your* uniqueness to go through the *proper channels* to
change it. Man is meant to grow through interaction with
others. If you are truly following your uniqueness, there
will be no need to destroy another. You will recognize that
you are part of an integral puzzle, each piece equal, each
piece unique and necessary to create the whole.

Even though you are within the flow of the universe and
the culture, you may march to a different drummer. If you
are against everything that is already established, you are
going to be like salmon swimming upstream. Eventually,
they get upstream to mate, but many fall along the way
because they are going against the current. The natural
instinct is to get there. It would be so much easier if you
could swim downstream. You have to permit yourself to
realize that, at times, when you feel totally boxed in, totally
frustrated, totally unable to move, you have to ask yourself
why. Perhaps in the effort to express your uniqueness, you
are losing sight of the whole picture. The full change seems
too overwhelming. It may be necessary to bridge to it gradually, accepting small changes toward it. Use your special

qualities to enhance things and help them move forward rather than demand the center stage action immediately.

If you are an author who takes your manuscript to a publisher and are told the work is unacceptable, you react. That reaction touches you in two ways. It touches the reality of yourself and the ego personality of yourself. *You* choose which to listen to. If you take the "how dare you" attitude and refuse to budge, you are going against the flow, and you will have a hard time. That is not your *uniqueness* talking, that is your *ego* talking. If instead you ask what it is that is unacceptable, you will find out what the problem areas are. Whether or not you will accept that as reality for yourself is entirely up to your free will. The ego has to be put aside so you can look at the facts.

Recognize that that does not mean that the publisher is totally right; but unless you are willing to listen, you may never get the foot in the door which will allow you to show your talent. You may think this is a compromise. Yes, in a way it is, but it is a compromise that is productive and active, not a compromise that is demeaning. If you were to step *back in time* and produce some of the literature that is in your world today, it would be totally unacceptable. What brought it to acceptability today? It moved forward by writing what *was* acceptable with just *enough* change to bridge the way. It is this way with everything in life. Along the way, you must merge the reality of where you *are* with where you *want to go*. Don't let ego become a barrier.

Ego is important. It gives you impetus; but if you let it rule everything, you may find yourself closing doors upon yourself instead of opening them. You are unique; there are no two souls alike. There are similar energy packages, but the special uniqueness of yourself has to be expressed and has to be fulfilled. You must function within the energy of the particular point of time you are in. Instead of running away when it does not seem to be going your way, tread water for a time and re-evaluate not *what* you are trying to do, but *how* you are trying to do it, for therein lies the tale. It is not that the belief is erroneous, but the manner in which it is being broached.

What makes you different? What makes you special? Your uniqueness rests in the quality and integration of your mind, body, and spirit. When these are in balance, you function through the Universal Laws. These give you clarity. Universally, by the Law of Polarity, there must be a point of the opposite in each thing. Therefore, in the negative, or that which appears to be negative, there has to be a point of positive that you can look for and use.

There are times when you feel denied. You feel that you are not getting where you want to go; you feel that you are not getting what you want to have. Recognize that there is truly a time for all things, *including* the unfoldment of the self. If you do that, you will be able to see that what you think of as a denial is probably a delay. If you accept that it is all right to have that delay, you will find yourself focusing more and more toward future achievements. Too often a person tries something; and if it doesn't work out, they drop it. It did not work; nobody would listen to them; it is over. No. If it was not heard or understood, perhaps it was not being approached in the right manner; perhaps it was not quite yet the time for it to be. Instead, look at it from another direction and give it another try. He who refuses to try a second time is denying his unique ability to be, for in each of you is success.

Most people think of success as reaching the top. It looks very glamorous and does not seem to take much effort. How wrong! It is usually a challenge all the way. In the process, people get so caught up in grasping at the goal that they resent the effort needed to get there. Take time to see the progress along the way, and you will see it as accomplishment. If you take time to see the peripheral that is learned and experienced every step of the way, you will understand that what seems to be a denial of your uniqueness is, in reality, an awakening of *all* the facets and *all* the perspectives of that uniqueness.

I have heard people say, "I was forced to do this; but through it, I found a part of me I didn't know existed. I found out that I can handle people very well." This is an expansion of the uniqueness of the individual. Later, what was learned in that forced issue will assist them in other goals.

Very often, man, because he is so attuned to getting there, does not bother to look out the window as he goes. During the journey to your goal, recognize that you are interacting with many people and incidents. Enjoy them and learn from them because they are as important to you as the goal itself. Those interactions give you the opportunity to hone your skills and evaluate your goals. You have to understand that there is sometimes friction, and there are sometimes steps backward instead of forward. Have you ever found yourself unsure of your footing? When you took a step backward, the next time you stepped forward, you were sure footed. It is no different in the travel of the soul. There are times when you are forced to stand still, or step back, but it does not mean that you are not moving ahead. You are getting a better grip on it, so to speak, a better footing. Remember, a better footing can mean *different* timing, a time which permits everything to flow smoothly. What I am asking you to do, in reality, is to take time to see *where* you are, where you *want* to go, and *why* you want to go. If you can answer those three things, you will know if you have chosen wisely. If you aren't willing to understand the path you are on, you are never going to have fulfillment from it.

Remember that the only absolute is change. Just when you think you are there, the mind and the inner uniqueness is going to sound again, and you are going to look for another aspect of life to achieve. You have success, but why only one in life, why not many? Focus on another aspect of yourself and let that grow.

There are times that because of life's complexities, you will find yourself forced to accept challenges that normally you would not want to accept. By working with those challenges, even though you dislike them, you may find a satisfaction in them. Sometimes you get to enjoy the challenge. You learn that you can face the challenge and overcome it. Even if you never go back to that particular thing again, you know that you can cope. Those challenges, those things you were forced to do, are very often there to let you be awakened to some quality within you that you have not been fully aware of.

Everyone likes to be in a safe place. Everyone likes to

know that they can go somewhere and be totally accepted. This can create a person dependent on *acceptance* for fulfillment. That, in turn, becomes fear of trying unless guaranteed a safe and comfortable space. Every once in a while, you have to step beyond that safety circle; but if you are truly centered, you will bring the quality of that circle with you and be able to create that sense of safety wherever you are. It is the difference between eating someone else's recipe and learning how to make it yourself. In the beginning, you taste something someone else has produced and you like it. Then one day you learn to make it yourself. That means you can still go back and enjoy theirs, but it also means the fear of being without it is gone. You can take it with you and create it yourself. It gives you a space in which to grow, strengthen, comprehend, and then to move on, not deserting the original goal, but expanding it and letting it be the true reality.

There are times when you will come upon someone who seems to be drifting without direction or control. They seem to be drifting without a rudder, unable to achieve. When a person is without a rudder, they should simply make a list of things they can do, close their eyes, pick one, and then work to achieve it. What they have to do is achieve at *something*. A person can tell themselves and others how they cannot get anywhere, how nothing is breaking for them, but they have never thought about *what it is* they want to break. They need to focus on *something* to prove to *themselves* that they are a productive being. The moment they have achieved at one productive thing, they will want another. From that, will come focus and realization of their own abilities. You can sit and say it's not happening; but until you stir your energy, it cannot happen . The person who wants to have a good job in a certain field knows there are certain things he must do to get there. He must be willing to learn thc skills that go with it. He must be willing to put effort and energy into it. He must be willing to go out and look for it.

If you do not extend energy to accomplish, you will not know how to do it. In other words, if you do not know how to be responsible, you cannot handle responsibility. You have to permit yourself to learn in small ways that later lead you to greater issues and fulfillment. When a person has a sense of having no direction, they must simply *take* a direction—any positive direction—and let themselves see success come from it. This will let them experience achievement. That achievement will, in turn, encourage them to further successes.

If you were to sit and never move, you would soon begin to atrophy. You would not know how to move; you would begin to forget how to make it happen. After a while, you would not even be able to focus on what moving was. Energy must move to manifest. When an opportunity is offered, you must act upon it and stir its energy in order to make it productive.

There are many factors that determine how a person will look at life. Because every person is unique, they use their own focus. Each energy looks at life in a different way. One person will want to know what makes it tick, why it is there, and will be very methodical in their thinking patterns. Others will want to experience everything and only then think about what to do with it. One is not better than the other; it is according to the individual's nature.

However, *action is the only thing* that can make something materialize, and *action that is focused* has the strongest materialization value. Thus, a form of focus needs to be there to make it happen.

If people are perfectly happy having nothing happen in their lives, that is fine, provided they are not imposing that on someone else. If they never want to work, if they want to sit and do nothing and never want to use their ability, that is their free will decision. God granted them free will, and there would be nothing wrong with it *provided* it did not affect others. It then becomes karmic, and it is an imposition that they will answer to in some form.

There are people who say, "I'm a gypsy at heart; I travel all over and I visit all my friends, and it's marvelous." It may be marvelous for them, but how about the friends that are feeding and housing them all of their lives? If the friends do not mind it, fine. However, the same amount of energy that is used to be indolent could be used constructively. It takes a lot of energy to worry about where the next meal is coming from. Many are put in that position not wanting to be there, and they are working very hard to try to change it, while others make it a way of life.

Anyone who sits and says, "Nothing is happening for me and nothing ever will," is not trying to do anything to make it happen. This individual is accepting and projecting failure by the repeated statement, "Nothing is happening for me and nothing ever will." People sometimes have fantasies about achieving. They are not ready to take responsibility for the dream goal. They make no effort to make it real, yet they insist that it is not happening because of other people or bad luck. The truth is, it is just that—a fantasy.

Your attitude affects your outcome. For instance, if you did not get a particular job, your own disappointment can cause you to magnify things and make you want it to be someone else's fault. It is easy to blame it on racism or someone else's attitude. These are labels pasted on empty jars. There is no content. Instead, ask yourself if perhaps somebody else was more qualified for the job. Did you really have everything you needed to qualify? If not, find out where you can get what you need so you are ready for the next job offer. You have to realize that labels are escape routes that, when used, can cause you to stop trying.

Uniqueness knows no race, color, or gender. It exists in everyone. However, if you have not discovered your specialness, you may feel insecure at times and feel the need to be defensive. But defensive against what? Logically, it would not be against the fact that someone else had trained for a position. That would not make sense. More logically, it would be against your own fears and doubts that you have built within. These fears can lead to an unbalanced approach to change of any kind, whether it be in you or around you. You can feel such a need to defend your present space that you create conflict and friction.

A conflict exists presently between the medical profession and the holistic healers, and until they both start giving in, no one is going to benefit. This conflict exists between male and female. What is wrong with being a female? Femininity is lovely, but it has nothing to do with ability. Masculinity is great, but it has nothing to do with ability. You have a mind and a soul coupled with the desire to grow. The

build of the body itself says that at some point it is not logical
for a female to do a certain thing, and perhaps it is also not
logical for a male to do certain things—*by logic alone,*—
having nothing to do with racism, or feminism, or anything
else. The power you give to anything comes from *within* you.
If a word bothers you, question why. It can only threaten you
if you accept it as a threat.

This is a time of change in your world. What you do with
it will either destroy you, or move you ahead. Do not use it as
an escape route from being you. Change always creates confusion. The inner need for change creates the action to world
change. If this is approached with a war-like attitude, rather
than an attitude of acceptance, it becomes more difficult.
Remember, change is progress. Use the energy of change to
move ahead.

The energy surrounding the soul is molded into a personality package by your free will. That energy is the energy you need to express yourself and work within the frame-
work of your uniqueness. How you build it and shape it is
up to you. In every instance, there are learning patterns that
go with that particular energy.

There are many persons who, for a variety of reasons,
never seem able to make a decision or choose a path. The
source of indecision is insecurity and lack of faith in the
self. It can also be fear of a wrong decision. There are no
wrong decisions. It is only what you do with it that makes it
either a positive or a negative thing. When a decision is
made, use it to gain something. If you feel another decision
might have been better, use the decision you have already
made first. Get all you can from it by learning from it. Give

it all you can to grow from it. Then you can decide what to do next. Wasting energy lamenting a possible error gets you nowhere. The point to realize is this: It is better to make *some* move than to make *no* move. You can analyze a decision for the rest of your life and never make it, or you can say, "This is the best I see; I'll take it and run with it."

Most people have the idea that if they make a decision to take a direction in life, they are never going to be able to do anything else. The only absolute is change. If you make a decision to try something and it is not what you want, there is nothing to say that you cannot make another decision. *Put effort into it.* While some people may be too willing to make a decision, or too fast in deciding without properly analyzing it, others analyze their whole life away and never make a move. There is nothing that cannot be changed in life—nothing—as long as you are willing to work at it.

Integration with others can sometimes create inner friction. There can be a feeling of being lost in the shuffle, or of being imposed upon. If you remember that everyone is approaching whatever it is through their energy and viewpoint, you will feel less threatened. To achieve group endeavor *all* viewpoints must be heard and considered. Consensus can then decide the direction to take. Permit your own uniqueness to be expressed in a pleasant way. Do not see another suggestion as war. Remember, only *you* can decide *what's right for you*, but in group goals, everyone has to work together. There are times when your uniqueness must work within outside direction. That does not make less of you unless you determine it does and accept it as your reality. For instance, if I choose to be judgmental, I need to know that I am going to be judged by the Universal Law of Cause and Effect in some way. If I choose to be constantly judgmental of others, I also have to accept that people may not like it, and I may find myself without too many friends around me. Then I have to ask myself, "Is that what I want? Is my focus taking me to a place that my reality does not really want? Should I be making alterations in myself along the way?

There are times, as you move to discover yourself, that anger, guilt, and even hatred will rise up within you. Remember, anger, hatred, and guilt are destructive forces after thirty seconds. Legally, you are allowed thirty seconds with those feelings. That is the natural defense mechanism of the body. At that point, *you decide* whether to make it an ego trip or whether to find out what it was in *you* that made it necessary and alter that in order to move on.

Anger, hatred, resentment, guilt, and fear are all emotionally bred, but they are all energy. To be non-fearful, you must take a step against fear. If you are afraid that you are not acceptable, then ask yourself what makes a person acceptable. Now ask what you can do as a first step toward becoming whatever it is. The first step toward that change is also a first step in *convincing yourself* that you are acceptable. You must take a logical step toward altering whatever it is you are fearing. Anger is telling you that there is something in you that is unable to accept what is happening, and you have to ask yourself why. The expression of emotion is a symptom of what is happening inside. Go inward and find the answer.

Experiences in life are sometimes like being tempered

by fire. They may seem negative at the time, but they are not. They give you the strength to make decisions about life. It is just as important to learn what you don't want in life as it is to know what you do want. Later you look back at the incident and realize what it taught. You may even realize that it saved you from something unproductive.

When you come together with others, you will often experience a yielding of your own desires in order to share a common space. This sharing and yielding is a free will action by you, and it is done not because of something that is imposed upon you, but from a desire to interact and enjoy what they have to offer you. This interaction is called synergy. Synergy is a form of compromise between two unique individuals, or a group of unique individuals. It is saying, "We have enough in common to find a place, or space, in which we can interact." Whenever you merge with another, you give something up, but you give it up out of your own desire, not out of somebody else's demand. You are not *losing* anything; you are *choosing* to do something. Do you understand the difference?

Everybody needs to be loved in some way, in some form. No one is so isolated a being that they do not need love or affection. You need one another. You even need those who drive you crazy, as you say in your world, because they are making you face a part of yourself by making you come to grips with attitudes and exchanges.

Many love associations develop a dependency factor. That occurs when you start permitting the interaction with another to become everything. By becoming too tied to another, you make it something to lean on. Because change is the only absolute, the association must grow, alter, and be experienced in many ways. You need to retain your identity within *any* interaction with others. You create common ground, but you do not become a shadow figure.

A perfect example of this: A group of people grow up together. They are childhood "buddies." They go through all their early school years together, and then they all go off to college. When they come back from college, there are still areas where they can get together and be buddies. Because they have all been in another learning experience, they can compare their college experiences. After they come out of that situation, they move into work patterns. Some marry, some do not. Different work patterns change the energies. Marriage and non-marriage make different energies. These buddies can now come together and go back and talk about high school or grade school and some of the college; but after a while, they begin to see that their friendship has changed. It has not become negative, it has altered in energy because each, in his own uniqueness, has been growing. The dependency on total sameness is exchanged for sharing diverse experiences. These friends now are enriching each other through differences instead of sameness.

Many years ago, a female married for the protection and support of the male. I am not saying they did not love each other, but they were in a point in time where both were accepting those roles as normalcy. Today you are in a point of change. While you will still be male or female by gender, there will be a desire to express the polarity of your gender. The female will no longer play a weaker role, but will desire to express her strength. She will no longer be afraid to be strong. The male will seek to express the gentle side of himself, recognizing it as a true strength. From this balancing of energies will come greater fulfillment and a deeper sense of well being. Whenever there is change, there is a period of time when there is conflict as adjustment creates a new space in which to interact.

A MEDITATIVE EXERCISE

Sit quietly, take a deep breath, and let yourself relax.

Think about yourself as you are *right now*. Look at yourself. See how you look and how you feel. See whether you smile or frown when you do it. Let yourself *really* think about you.

Now think about yourself as a many layered being and begin to peel away the layers of you. Take off the outer surface of yourself and look inward. Free yourself from the facade you hide behind. Let go of that outer reality you show to others. The hard shell dissolves now and you become a softer being.

Now peel away another layer of yourself and become aware of the vibration of yourself. Become aware of your own energy. You are no longer a facade, you are no longer hard-shelled. You are made malleable and pliable *by you*.

Peel still another layer away. Become aware of your own inner light. See it and feel it. You are no longer a facade, you are no longer hard-shelled, and you become more than malleable and pliable by you. You have begun to be able to see the *reality* of you. Permit yourself to enjoy it.

Now look at that light, soft, pliable, malleable you and realize that *you can now mold you*. Take the attitudes you wish were within you, the directions and focuses you want to have there, and place them deep within the light of you. Think of them clearly and precisely as you accept them as yours. Mind rules matter—as you think, so shall it be.

Breathe deeply and affirm this statement:
I accept my change.
I direct my change.
I know it has occurred.

Let yourself again see that soft light body you have become. Feel your vibratory rate increase. Permit that light vibration to literally burn away the old blockages.

Accept that *nothing* can keep you from becoming what you wish to become. *You* have burned away all blockages, all density that blinds.

You are now functioning in pure light that is the essence of your being, pure light that lets your creative self flow, be, and expand. You are love and light and joy, able to focus, move, and expand. You can *never* cease to use the potential you have accepted now. Your ability to function as you wish to function, in the manner that is helpful and wholesome to you, is now a deep-seated realization.

Take a moment to see light and feel love. Wrap your arms around yourself and feel love *from you to you*. Feel it penetrating you as you accept yourself as a *loveable* and *loving* being. Realize that the Creator and you are One. That High Self will now direct you as you permit yourself to accept love. Believe in you and trust your inner being.

Now take a deep breath and permit yourself to cover that body with a protective shield of light. You are a loving, trusting being protected by White Light that you may call upon at any time. You have protection from the crass world, but you are no longer hard-shelled. You are *not* vulnerable, you are *protected*, but you are aware of the beauty, light, and loving being that you are. Accept it.

Take a deep breath and permit your new self to emerge and be.

Through self-visualization and self-awareness, you have now taken away the defense mechanisms that block you. You have gone inward and planted a seed, and you have nurtured that seed and let it come to fruition.

Should you feel teary-eyed during this experience, accept it. Tears are not negative. They are a purging of sadness, anger, and guilt. Never be afraid to let them out, whether you be female or male, because they are a healthy release.

Recognize that permitting the unique individual in you to flow, does not have to be a grandiose thing. You are able to move forward more and more by letting the inner self gain control. Do not try to make it a quantum leap. Take it a step at a time in the small ways of life. Stay in touch with that inner you, and you will be led every step of the way.

Trust sets in motion the belief needed for manifestation.

CHAPTER II

SELF-ESTEEM

What is self esteem? It is to honor the self. Many people confuse self-centeredness with self-esteem, but they are two entirely different things. Self-esteem is the acceptance of the potentials and qualities of the self. Self-esteem permits you to be proud of your accomplishments without being self-centered or selfish. Without self-esteem, one is inclined to belittle their potentials and qualities and to feel less than they are. This creates a lethargy that keeps them from using those qualities that can give them the very thing they are looking for—belief in self.

One of the things you must be very sure about is what "self" means. What does "self" mean? Does self mean the ego-personality aspect or the reality aspect, which is the higher part of you? Self is the combination of the two. There is the tendency by many to throw the baby out with the bath water by thinking you cannot use your ego or your personality because it makes you less saintly. Instead, recognize that when self-esteem is present, the *full* realization of the self is present. Thus the higher part of you can keep the ego-personality in a fine and perfect balance.

Recognize that you are not here to be anybody else but *you*. Tall people want to be short, and short people want to be tall. People who are too thin wish to be heavy, and those who are too heavy wish to be thin. Many people can go on and on about all the things they do not like about themselves. Accept the fact that you are here to be you, no matter what color, no matter what hair, no matter what height you are. These features have nothing to do with the quality aspect of you. You are here to be you, and you are here to be the *best you* that you can possibly be.

What part of you is not being used, or fulfilled, at the moment? You may need to stimulate the mind more, or perhaps you have to pull away from thinking so much and start doing something physical. Only when you know the full potential of you can you possibly have a sense of well-being about yourself. As long as you are feeling that there are parts of you not being fulfilled, you will have a sense of being less than your full potential.

Self-esteem is not something that you accomplish and then rest upon as a plateau. As long as you live, as long as you are dealing with moving, growing, and evolving, there will always be the challenge of greater accomplishment. This will give you the opportunity to achieve and feel even better about yourself. The one thing you have to understand is that self-esteem can never be achieved by lassitude, lack of application, or refusal to try. You cannot sit and wait for someone to deliver it; you have to seek it. Most people seek answers out in the world. There attitude is: *World, recog - nize me; world, tell me I'm okay, tell me I'm good, tell me something.* Instead you have to go inside. Ask the high part of you to tell you what you need to know. You will express and achieve through the outer world, but you will be directed from within.

As you are focusing on self-esteem and its development, I want you to think briefly about areas you do not feel good about within yourself. There are many areas where people feel stuck. As we go on with this material, some of the common areas will come to light. Look to see where these or similar areas might be an area you wish to work with. A common sticking point with many is lack of focus, beginning too many things and then not finishing them, or perhaps finishing only one or two. Focus is necessary for achievement. If you scatter the energy and the focus, you will not have enough energy to achieve in any one place. There are times when you get an idea or become excited about doing something but later find that that interest isn't sustained by the actual participation. The tendency then is to drop it. That can leave you with a feeling of incompleteness and the feeling that you must do something else in its place. Too many such experiences may make you doubt your ability to do anything.

Sometimes a person will start multiple things because it makes them feel clever. There is nothing wrong with that. It is clever that you have four, five, or six ideas; but if you have four, five, or six ideas, then you are too busy having ideas to do anything about them. You can begin to see how things sneak up on you. Eventually, when nothing seems to come to fruition, frustration starts and you feel let down.

Look at the projects that you are thinking about and prioritize them by value or importance. When you accomplish what *has* to come first, even if it is the one you like the least, you will have such a good feeling about it that you will be motivated to move on to accomplish the next one. The only way you are going to do it is to shorten your leash. This will allow you to accomplish within that project's range, and then you can move on to something else.

If you are working with something where you are doing the same thing constantly, if there is no variation within the work pattern, very often boredom will set in. This creates a lassitude. A sense of *I don't feel like being creative any - more* is felt.That is a trap that you can fall into, so you must always be sure that you are giving yourself enough stimulation in addition to your regular activity. If you are in a very creative field, learn something of a technical nature. Take up an activity which separates you from your work. Go out and run. Do something that takes you away from what you do all the time. This will help to balance you out.

There are many times when you are faced with learning a new task or job. Let us use as an example learning to drive a car. To someone who has never driven one before, it may represent a tremendous challenge. It is a task which could cause them to feel fearful. Because fear creates barriers to learning, it becomes necessary to make the process less fearful. You have to overcome the fear. When you think of the whole package, it seems too overwhelming. Break it down to steps that you can handle.

The first thing you need to do is become familiar with a car. *Anything that you understand is not as fearful a thing.*

Find out what makes it tick. Take a course, if necessary. It is the unknown that is fearful. Permit yourself to know the car. Then ask a friend to take you someplace where you can get out into a big field. Go to some farm where there are farm roads and start driving your machine there where you have nothing to run into. Get the feel of the machine. Gradually, it will become easier.

When a baby is learning to walk, you do not stand them up at the head of the stairs. You put them in a safe place. Do the same with yourself. As you begin to feel a sense of being in control, you will begin to become comfortable with the machine. As you become comfortable with it, you can then begin to learn what else you need to know in order to take your lessons further. As you become familiar with the car, your sense of achievement and fulfillment will soon overcome the fear.

Always remember, you cannot go from A to Z without understanding and going through all the other letters in the alphabet. In learning any new task, you move from a point of what you know and are capable of to the area where you wish to accomplish. You have to bridge between those two places. Take what you have at the point you are in right now and use it joyously. When you have seen the results of that, when fulfillment has come from it, you will find that you are able to move forward, and you will have accomplished all along the way as well.

You can frame and hang all the certificates on the wall you want, but if you are not using and sharing what you were taught, you have not learned. If you are in the process of getting an education, ask yourself why you are getting it.

Is it really serving that which you truly desire to do? Many people approach education as a check list, never stopping to identify with it along the way. This does not demean education. Your mind needs stimulation and excitement, but it also has to be in balance with the rest of you in a manner that allows you to productively *use what you know now* in order to learn more.

The moment you reach a point where the fulfillment factor begins to dim, it is time to go for another step in fulfillment. It means your potential is ready for something new. Therefore, you have to alter things in some way through a new or parallel application of what you are now doing.

The time you are living in right now is both difficult and exciting. The only thing that is absolute now is change. Nothing can remain stagnant. Movement is always going to be there. No matter what you achieve, you are going to know inside that there is more to achieve. This will not take away the fun of achieving and, perhaps, will stimulate many who would not otherwise seek to grow. That sense of discontent is the catalyst that moves you.

Very often people who are quite creative—artists, actors, and the like—will seem to suffer periods of little or no creative energy. If they are not using that potential and bringing it out to share, they feel lost. It is then that they rely on inner belief. Self-esteem tells them that this is only a pause in their career. If it is moving slowly, recognize that it *is* moving. Accept that it will accelerate.

Along the way, you gain confidence by your participation, your training, and your work. You begin to believe in your ability. Sometimes you may begin to be fearful that something will come along and upset the apple cart. These thoughts can put pressure on you. If you are *achieving*, it is because you have *earned* it.

There is often confusion about self-esteem, loving the self, and loving others. Self-esteem is believing in yourself and accepting that *you* are in control of *you* no matter what is going on. It is respecting who you are and has nothing to do with education, wealth, occupation, or social level. It is the God-given power of you. You express it through *your* value system and your *chosen* standards. When you are in touch with that inner higher self, you *do* like and love yourself. It is not the self-loving of a self-centered person. Self-centered love is not the balanced acceptance of who you are, but rather an all consuming self-importance. That is not the love we are talking about in reference to self-esteem.

As you grow, you develop standards by which you then live. When you are using them correctly, you sense that things are right for you, and you are comfortable. If, however, you find yourself straying from them, you may begin to feel uneasy. When that happens, check out why you are feeling that way. You will soon have things under control again. Remember, you are expressing *your* self-esteem and standards, *not someone else's*.

Learning to feel good about yourself permits you to interact as yourself without fearing others opinions about you. You are less apt to feel dominated or taken advantage of. *In other words, you will not lose your identity when interacting with others*. If someone's only identity is to be the nice guy who takes care of everything for everybody, he will soon feel several things: 1, He will begin to feel used; 2, he will resent that and feel angry; and 3, hc will feel lost because he has begun to think that that is what he has to be in order to be accepted.

There is often confusion about bragging and having self-esteem. It is quite acceptable to claim your own abilities, that is self-esteem. Having no conversational ability other than that is ego. Self-esteem states your ability; ego says you're the only one with the ability. To "toot your own horn" means accepting your qualities, not as a *special* thing, but as a *natural* thing.

How can you help yourself realize when your self-esteem is lowering? There are many ways in which you can check and guide yourself along the way. As you pass a store window, take a glance at yourself. What is your posture like? Are your shoulders back? Are you in love with the world? It will shock you, because most people do not realize how they reflect their inner feelings through their posture. It starts with the head hanging low, the shoulders slumping, the spine curving, and you look like the letter "S."

After you have begun to notice how you carry yourself, the next aspect to pay attention to is your voice. Every once in a while, listen to your voice. There are tell-tale signs in the tone you use. Is your voice going up an octave at a time as you proclaim your miserable day? Is your voice becoming a whine? Is it lowering to an unintelligible whisper that announces fear of not being worth listening to? Is it becoming loud and angry in tone? You may be quite surprised at how you really sound. Pay attention to what you say and how you think. Your frame of mind is important. Watch out! These are warning signals to you. They are saying you are losing your belief in *you* and in your potential and in your ability.

Another area that is often neglected is physical appearance. *I've only worn this shirt four days; it ought to do one more day.* Heaven help the person sitting behind or downwind of you. When you begin to let yourself become slipshod about your dress, you are beginning to let go of your belief in you. You are beginning to not care how you express yourself outwardly. Watch your voice, watch your posture, and watch your facial expressions. These are all important indications of what is going on in you.

You will feel wonderful no matter where you are if you are feeling good about yourself. If you live in a crowded city where there are multiple energies, multiple mental attitudes, multiple businesses and standards, and multiple cultures, that too is an education. Every time you say a place is terrible, stop and look about and try to learn something from it and realize what it is giving you.

When you seek to develop self-esteem, you use the world as a mirror of your own ability. As you begin to accept the quality of yourself, your work improves. It will be accepted more fully. No matter how many times you seek a favorable opinion from another, it will not give fulfillment unless *you yourself* believe it. Understand that does not mean that you are going to be the prima ballerina, or the greatest author in the world, but your work will be recognized, and you will feel good about it. If you spend all the time lamenting the fact that you are not there yet, you have no energy to get there.

Start with your vocabulary. Are your words self-deprecating? When you are trying to reach a goal, your thoughts and words need to bridge from where you are to where you're going. Let your words flow between the spaces. Whatever you are trying to achieve or bring into your life may call for releasing something already there. Periodically check on what is *not* serving you well in life. Then ask what would best replace it. Begin to move toward it in words. If at first you can't be positive, then at least don't be negative. Instead of saying it can't work, say maybe it can. At least it leaves the door open to possibility. Later you might want to let "maybe" become "it will." The words you use are the keys to what is happening in your life. Some words are binders, and some words are gates. The phrase "I hope" leaves room for doubt. Say "I know," "I can," "I will." "I *will* be the best of me I can possibly be, because I *want* to, not because I *have* to." Do you see the difference?

Decisions are necessary for change to occur, and everyone is faced with making them daily in many areas of their lives. A person who feels they should be earning more money than they are at their present job, must make a decision. They must first examine the present job and what they do to merit their pay check. Now the decision can be made to either request more money for services rendered, or to look for a different job that will pay more. To simply sit and have a temper tantrum about the situation you are in presently serves no purpose. Learn from where you are, re-evaluate, and move on.

If you take the paycheck for the job, you have accepted the rules and regulations of the job. If you have to be there at nine, then you know you had better get up early enough to get there at nine. You can not say your standard is to get there at ten. That is ego. That has nothing to do with a standard. Watch that you are not confusing the ego-personality aspect with a standard. A standard will never hurt you if it is *your* standard, and you are living by it. The important question is whether or not you are doing a good job.

Know that in your development, the very worst that can happen to you is that you might make a mistake. Heaven forbid you never made a mistake in your life! What a boring life you would have! Do you know that you learn more by your mistakes than anything else? You call it "the school of hard knocks." The thing to remember is that a mistake is not the end of the world; it does not mean you are a lesser person. It means that you made an error that you have recognized, learned from, and can now amend.

All advancement in any form must have a foundation to move from. Everything is built layer by layer, readiness by readiness. When you are trying to do something you are not ready for, you are nervous and up tight and are more apt to make a mistake. Be secure where you are and *then* move forward. In order to be secure where you are, you have to *accept that it is okay* to be where you are. You have to stop fighting it and stop making it an enemy. Instead, start liking it and making it an asset. Learn to like where you are for what it is teaching you, even though, at the present time, it does not seem to be what you really want.

There is the false impression that in not promoting a

student, it will some how damage their self-esteem. It does not. They may feel disappointed about it at the time it occurs, but think of the other end of it. When a child does not have the foundation for more advanced work, he is frustrated and becomes fearful. If they are promoted along with their friends who are able to go ahead and do the more advanced school work, then their every moment in that new environment is going to be miserable. In many ways they have been done a tremendous disservice, because now the anger of their inability to compete in the new level of work will be coupled with whatever caused them to fall behind in the first place. The degree of disappointment a child feels when not promoted will be based on the attitudes of the *parents* and *other adults* involved. The adult attitude should be supportive, not demeaning.

If you have pushed to have your child promoted when maybe it was not the most appropriate decision, do not feel guilty about it. Remember what I said before. There is nothing wrong with mistakes as long as you learn from them. The thing you have to remember is that the *child* has to carry the load, not the teacher and not the parent. If you are putting so much attention on whether he is keeping up with Johnny, then your standards are based on what Johnny's parents are doing, and that means you do not have a standard of your own. Prepare your child adequately through special tutoring if you are going to have him promoted. Only then will you be doing what is best for the child.

No matter what age you are, if you approach a change insecurely, you are going to spend so much time on your insecurity that you are not going to gain fully from the move. You have to realize that you have to *prepare* for something. You have to know where you are headed, you have to know what you need to learn to get there, and you have to be *willing* to get it. Do not expect it to come in the box of cracker jacks. Each case must be looked at individually, so ask yourself what is best.

Many people adopt habits which they feel are in vogue or "in" as a method of trying to bolster their self-esteem. Most people smoke because at a period of time it was the "in" thing, and it since has become a habit. It is used as a crutch in a tense moment. It is soothing, sort of like a pacifier. Everyone has different kinds of pacifiers in life. If you want to eliminate that habit, begin to prepare yourself. Let yourself begin to release the habit through your words. When you have a smoke, tell yourself that it doesn't taste the same. Choose a date months away and begin affirming that you will no longer desire to smoke by then. Those words bridge from where you are to where you want to be, they flow. When you claim you want to quit but can't you are defeating yourself before you begin. To claim you do not desire means its *your choice*, and the ego does not get upset or excited. If you claim you *can't have*, the ego goes berserk and holds you to the old pattern. Use both casual and strong positive statements toward your goal. If you feed those thoughts to the subconscious, it will, in turn, release a lack of desire for that particular thing. The subconscious rules the body through the pituitary gland. You gradually override the ego orientated conscious mind and let the suggestion to the subconscious do the reprogramming. That way you are not warring with the self. Respect yourself enough to be willing to try.

Stop for a minute and think about where you are and what you want out of life. Then make two lists. One will be what you have in your life at the present time, and the other will be where you want to go. Start using a vocabulary that flows toward those goals, not one that diminishes your ability to get there. A vocabulary that constantly says, "I can't," will close the door to your future. You must take logical steps toward that goal. The only way to build such a bridge is through thoughts and actions that permit you to flow toward it.

Many people have difficulty in developing a sense of self-esteem because they have viewed their behavior as being dependent on what they perceived as society's standards. Society is like the "they" that will not let you do things. Those mythical beasties, the "theys" and "the society." You have to look within yourself and decide what is right for you. How do you feel about risk-taking? Society can suggest taking a risk all they want; *they are not taking it—you are.* I can tell you that a full bottle of scotch is better than one sip, but I am not drinking it. You have to ask yourself by whose standard you are making this move. If you cannot say by your own standard, then do not take the risk.

Understand that in the development of self-esteem, self-trust and a realistic understanding of one's self takes time. It takes time, energy, and perseverance toward that goal. You will have to learn things along the way. There are levels you go through to get where you want to go. As long as you are willing to work with those levels, you will not be taking a risk. Always remember, you have the power to make it happen. You have the superconscious mind which knows where you are supposed to go. Trust it. Let it guide you.

You have to ask yourself if your goals are realistic. Are your goals fantasies or have you thought creatively about them? Fantasies let you play with an idea, but it remains a fantasy. You have moved nowhere with it. If you take that fantasy and make it a creative thing, you begin to think, "How could I make it happen?" What would I have to do? What would be the first step toward it? You come away with logical movements. The key is movement—movement toward the goal. You can spend your whole life fantasizing and never face reality once. You have to put fantasy into a creative flow which, in turn, will manifest through your own movement and action. You have spirit to help you, but *do not expect spirit to do for you what you will not do for yourself.* You must stir the energy. Then it becomes the magnet that pulls in the help you need. You cannot sit and say, "The good fairy is going to drop it on me." It does not work that way. You all have a side of you that is the pauper, and you all have a side of you that is the Prince. The side of you that is the pauper is that one that says, "I can't." "Today was a terrible day; I'm going to have a terrible night." In that space, you are poor in spirit.

Poor in spirit means unable to let the help come in. Focusing on all that is wrong with you instead of something that is right with you does not help. Know that where you use your energy is where the movement will occur. The prince in you is that side that says, "I know it can happen, because I am working at it." "I can." "I can have an excellent day; I control my destiny." In that space you are a wealthy person. You are recognizing that God is your source of all supply and that he will provide for you if you are willing to expend the energy yourself. You are focusing on what is *right* with you and on what you *can* do. If you are willing to work with the abilities that you have, you will, in turn, be guided to that which is right and proper for you. It is the element of trust and acceptance within that makes you a rich person. In that way, you are focusing on all that is right with you and on *all* that your potential is. You will, in that space, never be let down.

A person may have spent considerable energy focusing on a goal which they perceive as right and perfect for them. All along, day in and day out, the thought within was that this was a goal that they desired and felt was right for them. As time passed, the goal became a reality. The first reaction was one of surprise and fear. The fear represented a sense of uneasiness within because now the responsibility that went with the dream was real. They suddenly feel fearful. They then accept the new role and proceed. *Temporary* doubt is normal.

I want you to understand the process. First of all, the subliminal thought has been there all the time. It has been there in absolute faith, unfettered because you had accepted it. All the time it has been meaningfully working for you so that at its right and perfect time, it could enter your life when *you were ready* for it. You have been dreaming about it long before you were ready for it. The dreaming of it kept you in readiness to take the logical steps toward it. Do not be afraid of it now. Do not start looking at what is missing. Realize that this is the effect of your cause. The cause of belief created the effect which says it is here. Go for it. Above all, recognize that *you deserve it.*

Very often when something you have wanted comes to you, the panic sets in. *Now I've got it; now I've got to prove myself. Now I've got to be bigger than anything I've ever been before.* Again, *you* are putting yourself on trial. Approach it with joy. Approach it with the realization that whatever work has to go with it, you will do. If necessary, you will learn what you need to know and make that experience a joyous one. Remember, if it has manifested in your life, you have earned it.

Self-esteem comes from the fulfillment of accomplishment, and it does not matter whether it is doing the windows in the apartment, getting a new job, or having a new relationship. It is something that fulfills a part of you and makes you feel good.

The joy of this new Age is that it is a time of release. You need not stay in one vocation forever as you used to in the Piscean Age. In this Age, movement and flow says: When I have achieved in one area, if I *want* to move to another, there is nothing wrong with that. I don't have to think I'm 'copping out,' or that I am failing.

Very often a person will get an idea based on some obscure thing, and they make that a goal in their life. If that goal is made as a child with a child's view, heaven only knows what you are setting yourself up for. A child may see a limousine and decide that that is what they want to have. They want to have a big limousine. In town, the only one who owns a limousine is the undertaker so the association says: I'm going to be an undertaker, because then I'll have a limousine. That sounds ridiculous, but that is what happens sometimes. It is necessary to periodically check where a dream or goal comes from. Just as you grow to become an adult, your dreams and goals must also grow.

Always look at the polarity of it, what goes with it, because once you make a decision, you get the whole package. There are no half packages; there are no wrong decisions; but you get the whole package of whatever decisions you make. Along the way, you have to question whether it fits your life now. Is there something you would rather be doing now? Is there something that will give you a greater sense of your own potential and well-being if you were to look in a different direction?

You can only move forward by letting go of something. All advancement is based on sacrifice. You give up childhood to become an adult; you give up one station in life to assume another; you give up your single state to be married; and you give up time and energy to be a parent. You give up something to gain something else. Why? Because it is necessary to release those things that are no longer serving you at that particular point in your life.

It begins with attitudes and perspectives. Your attitudes as a swinging single are quite different from what they are when you meet the right person. You let go of those attitudes in order to enhance the new ones that will come with marriage. You can't handle the responsibility of the two places, so you carry what is healthy and helpful forward and let go of the rest. You don't negate what was before; you thank it for what it gave you and move on. Periodically check your progress. See if you are placing yourself in overload by not releasing that which doesn't fit.

When trying to decide a direction or a standard, be aware of your feelings. When something does not feel right, take another look. Ask yourself why you are feeling unsure about it. You have to be willing to look inward at what is making you drag your feet.

Suppose you have lost your sense of direction? When you are not really sure if what you are doing is right, start examining where you are. If you are not happy in the space you are in, you have to ask yourself why. You have to be willing to turn around and face the tiger. Only *you* can make you happy, only *you* can make you angry, and only *you* can make you sad. For instance, I can tell you you are a funny person, I don't like you, and I think you're dumb. If you *accept* what I have said, then you are. Listen to what is said, but check its reality in relationship to you. You have to ask yourself, "Why am I not happy right here where I am?" Examining why you are not happy will help you understand your situation.

A lot of people say they are not happy, but they do not want to find out why. Go through your day; go through your life; go through your associations and be willing to search for an answer. Ask yourself when this happens, when do you have this feeling? Then investigate why. You are going to find out what it is you need to know to make where you are *right now* a happy space. From there, take that happiness forward. Ask yourself how much of your unhappiness comes from your rigidity or inability to see another person's viewpoint. The change really has to come from where you are right now. You do not find it by running to someplace else. If you do not know why you are unhappy here, you will not know why you are going to be unhappy elsewhere. Be willing to look at the ingredients you are working with right now. Find out what it is that makes you unhappy right now. You will find that insecurity in an area

41

creates a feeling of inadequacy in you. Recognize that you do not have to know everything or experience everything others have. Some people will be nervous about being with people who are very knowledgeable, or who are well traveled. They will feel inadequate with them. They have to ask themselves what difference it makes. Do not let what others are limit what you think of yourself.

Everything in life that affects you has two sources, one, where *you* are coming from, and two, where society is coming from. Often one confuses what they are supposed to respond to. Remember that the first source you respond to is *you*. You are here to be you, to be happy as you, and to find your potential and self-esteem as you. You were not to be as the man down the street, or the woman across the way. You have to stop trying to compare yourself to others and start asking yourself, "What do I want to do with my life; what do I want to change *within me* so that I feel secure and comfortable?"

Many people confuse the need for money with self-esteem. It is nice to have money, your world works on money, and there is nothing wrong with money. If you do not have enough money to do all the things you want to do right now, don't start denying your right to it. Instead, touch it where you can. Read about it, talk about it, and treat it as if it is yours. You will then begin to find a means to open the doors that give you what you need. If you are saying, "I can't have it," it is already being denied you by *you*.. Spirit cannot act without your permission, and your permission comes through *you* stirring the energy and starting the movement that allows spirit to help you.

Write down goals and write down the things you want. As you move along, begin to trust yourself. Trust yourself to be fair with yourself, trust yourself to be honest with yourself, and be honest enough to say, "I've been barking up the wrong tree all the time." Be willing to change something. Be willing to ask if this is right for you *at this point* in your life. Do not think that changing your goals makes you a failure. That word "failure" is bandied about so much that everyone is afraid of it.

The only thing that people are more afraid of than failure is success, because there is a tremendous amount of responsibility that goes with success. There are degrees of success and success must fulfill you on all levels, or it is not success at all. Monetary return is nice, but it is not enough. There also has to be the joy of the heart and the contentment from within. You have to respect your ability and see it as wealth that can't be taken away from you.

You are full of potential. Think of yourself as being wonderful, divine children of the Creative Force with absolute perfection *right now*. Take that fuel and use it. Believe in you enough to let it happen for you. You beat yourselves to death; you put yourselves on trial. If you feel you are not enough, ask yourself why. Be willing to question yourself without guilt. He who discovers an error within and acts to alter it is wise. Be willing to learn what you need to do to move forward. Tell yourself that you *will* succeed. Permit yourself to see how wonderful you are.

We have established that self-esteem is built. Although you are born with the full realization of the quality and beauty of the self, it is not easily accepted by you as you begin to integrate into the physical world. As you move through life, you tend to pull away from your attunement to the reality of you and begin to accept the direction of the personality. As you do that, you begin to set your goals and objectives by the society's standard, by peer group pressure, and by what you feel *you ought to be*.

When you are a child and somebody tells you to set the table, you set the table because you know how to set the table and because it was asked of you. If, however, it is your idea to set the table, you set the table with a different attitude. You set it because you want to. You make sure that everything matches, that everything is the best you can possibly make it. It is an extension of you, a fulfillment of that which you have instigated or started. In life, the greatest fulfillment, the greatest sense of self-recognition or self-esteem comes from self-instigated direction. In order to have self-instigated direction, you have to know where you want to go. You have to have an idea of what it is you would like to bring into your life. In order to know what it is you would like to bring into your life, you have to look at the moment you are in. If you look back, you are going to try to see your value by what has been. What has been is a reflection of where *you were* in those past points in time. Where you are headed will be based on what you do with the points in time yet to be. If you look back and say, "I was successful here," you are liable to say, "I can be successful again." However, if you look back and say, "I didn't do that, this wasn't right," you can find a million reasons why you cannot succeed now. You must say, "No matter what has been before—good, bad, or indifferent—I can create a future that will fulfill me and let me believe in myself."

The key word is "self." The *self*. Who is going to experience it? The self. Who is going to be fulfilled from it? The self. You have to start where self can touch it at the moment. You have to be willing to say, "This is what I can do about it right now." This is the step I can take *right now*. It may not be the step that is the total fulfillment, but you have to see the *potential* of fulfillment from that step. He who wants to dance has to learn to dance. If he perceives his lessons and practice only as hard work, a drag, and a hassle, he is never going to be a good dancer. He is never going to have fulfillment, because fulfillment is built block by block. The first fulfillment occurs when the aches begin to subside. A step toward the goal has been conquered. By seeing the process as achieving the goal, it all becomes easier. The greater agility, the new routines, the new partners, and the opportunity to perform are all successes within the process of gaining the title "dancer."

Take a moment right now to ask yourself how you have ignored or refused to see fulfillment. There are very few people who have not done so in some way. Sometimes they are so subtle you do not see them easily. You have to grab those positive points and move forward with them. Do not permit yourself to fall into the trap of self-denial. Remember, when you succeed in catching a cab, it is the first fulfillment on your trip to where you are going. Do not see it as a struggle, but as an achievement.

When self-esteem is low, there can be the tendency to try to bolster it through acts outside the self, the "Look, I'm a good person because I'm giving up my apartment to help someone else" syndrome. There are times when it is easier to assist someone else to do something than it is to create something for yourself. You settle for peripheral fulfillment, that which says you were part of something in some way. While this feels good, it still leaves you feeling as if you might have cheated yourself.

There are times when somebody does need you, and you sacrifice something for them. An escape route through service very often says, "I can't put the time into me, because I have to put my time into someone else." You do it gladly. There is nothing wrong with that, but an escape route through service can be slipped into easily. It is an escape from making decisions about yourself. If someone always needs you, you don't ever have to make a movement of your own. Service is a wonderful thing, but you also have to be self-serving.

You hear statements that say, "I want peace. I want to be happy. I want to be healthy." They are wonderful goals, but where can you touch them right *now*. Peace is not outside yourself; it is inside yourself. Wealth is not outside yourself; it is inside yourself. Success is not outside yourself; it is inside yourself. You have to go inward and define what peace, wealth, and happiness is (to you) right now where you are today.

What is the first thing you do? If you are unhappy, why are you unhappy? Most people cannot tell you why they are unhappy. They can say, "I'm unhappy because the bus was late." "I'm unhappy because the dog wet on the floor." You are really unhappy for any number of things, but none of those reasons are why you are really unhappy. *You are unhappy because you are dissatisfied with the space you are in at that point in time*. To change those feelings you have to move your energy into a new space, so it can grow and move forward. If you do not like where you are, where do you want to go? If you do not like what is in your life now, what do you want to be rid of?

Movement is based just as much on letting go of things as it is on taking on things. Just as children outgrow shoes, you outgrow points in time when something is valid for you. You have to ask, "What is valid for me at *this point in time*, and what am I doing to make it happen?" Trust yourself enough to know that there is a move that you can make.

Many times a person will say, "This is what I want," and there they sit with it. They expect the good fairy to come and drop it down on their doorstep in the morning. Sometimes you have to ask what parallel energies are involved. What are the other ways that the same thing can be achieved. Sometimes you are trying to take a route that cannot get you there when an alternate route can. An alternate route to an achievement financially could mean working at something that is not exactly what you want in order to afford the training you want. You have to bless that work and thank it for the encouragement toward study which helps you to make the move to where you want to be.

In the structured life of the Piscean period, there were certain logical steps toward happiness. A child would grow, study and become productive in some way. Eventually they would seek a mate, marry, and have children. They would raise those children, and then those children would repeat that pattern all over again. If they have not taken the time to enjoy the study, the work, and their children along the way, they could not have a true sense of fulfillment. They would have gone through all the steps on the checklist, but they would not have felt fulfilled.

Fulfillment comes from movement, and it comes from the appreciation of each step of that movement along the way. The child that comes home so enthusiastic because they have learned to make an "A" has started building self-esteem. As he learns more and more letters, the self-esteem grows. Then he finds out that he can put them together, and they will say something. Those groups of words can become a story! What a magical feeling of power that can bring. If along the way they get no encouragement, they may begin to see it not as an achievement but as hard work or drudgery.

One of the worst offenses to children is not recognizing their need to *be exuberant* about the learning process. People will tell children they are stupid. A child might make mistakes, but that does not make the child stupid. If, however, you tell them they are stupid long enough, they will accept that and manifest stupidity.

Guilt lowers self-esteem. Have you ever felt guilty? Everyone at sometime feels that they have done something that somebody is not going to approve of. That does not mean that you have to assume that it becomes a living part of you for the rest of your life. Self-esteem is based on facing old guilt and letting it go, facing old attitudes—old angers and resentments—and letting them go. It is being able to say that no matter what happened in that point in time, in a new point in time, it can be different. You can move forward in whatever way you want to. You *can* achieve.

Confusion can be created by setting a single minded goal which has no alternatives and no parallel approaches. Logic says that unless you have the skills and preparation, you can't start at the top. The goal to make fifty thousand dollars a year, if you are not prepared, is, in effect, a single minded goal—I want fifty thousand, that's it. A parallel route would first suggest you make fifteen thousand a year and move up from there. The parallel route suggests you move up in ability and talent to eventually make fifty thousand. Self-esteem is in the belief that you *can* earn fifty thousand, but are willing to take joy in the fifteen, twenty, and twenty-five along the way. Otherwise you will think you are failing every day of your life if you are not making the fifty thousand. *Know* you *can* make it. You can build the trust in your ability to make it happen, but not by fantasizing. Make being realistic and flexible the first step in your self-esteem building.

What is it you think would make you feel good about yourself? Do not think about what other people say *should* make you feel good about yourself, but what *you* feel would make you feel good about yourself. Think about it a moment. If that is what will make you feel good about yourself, how many ways are there to go about it?

Let us suppose, as an example, you decide you want to start a learning center for children and older people. That decision calls for other decisions. Some questions you might need to ask yourself are:
1. What is the logical timing for this venture?
2. Where can I touch it now with the limited resources on hand?
3. What skills do I need to have in order to successfully venture into this? Where do I go to get them?
4. Is this something I want or something I *think* I should have?
5. Am I ready to assume this responsibility.
Perhaps the thing you want to do first is learn how to handle

money, since eventually it will take money to develop that goal. This would be a step toward your overall goal. Secondly, there are many homes for the aged in which there is no opportunity for communication with young children. There are many children's organization which are looking for contact with older people. A way to touch your goal *now* is to work as a liaison person between the two agencies and put them in touch with each other. The learning center has already begun. It can be touched now. It may not be identified as strictly yours, but you are putting the energy flow into motion. If you have one young child and one older person that you can bring together for an hour, you have already put the learning center into process. If the principle is workable, *work it where you can touch it* now. What you learn along the way will enhance the final achievement.

There is always a way to touch the ultimate goal *now*, and that is where you work with it. That gives the impetus to let it grow. Before you can afford to go to a school for fashion design, go out and look at fashion. It means learning to sew yourself. If you cannot be where you want to be, be in association with it in some way in the interim. Your self-esteem will be built as you realize there are multiple ways to touch it.

Suppose you want to work with drama and the healing arts. Healing takes place on many levels. Laughter is one of God's greatest gifts to mankind. Humor is the thing that can keep you from becoming totally unbalanced. If you can laugh at yourself in a situation, you will be able to come out of it. Drama, mime, and singing can be used as healing tools. Song is universal, music is universal, and dance is universal. They are all universal languages, They can easily be used as forms of healing. The question is: How do you get to that goal? What is it you have to learn along the way? You have to be willing to do your part. Do not be so busy bemoaning the fact that you are not up front, center stage, that you forget to perform in everyday life.

Learn that there are parallel roads and movements. Anything that is to take form, takes form on three levels. The first level is the movement within, the raw energy of its possibility and potential to be. That means a movement within your potential to bring it into fruition and a movement within the energy of that essence. The movement is started by *your* thought pattern and continued by *your* action.

The first place it is experienced is in the *idea*, the second place it is experienced is in the personal *action*, and the third and last place it is experienced is in the *fulfillment* of the dream. One step cannot come before the other. The birth of the idea needs your willingness to touch it where you are in order to move the energy toward its ultimate potential. Creative ether contains all things, and in you rests the potential to tap it. The universe is in *you*. When you let your own potential merge with that creative ether potential, new concepts are brought forth. An idea is born in you. Now you must express it *outside* of you. Bring it forth verbally to affirm it, trusting that it can be manifested. This leads to action upon it and fruition.

As it comes into fruition, it goes through stages of unfoldment. The flower does not become a full bloom without first being a bud. Anything that is growing has to start in a small space and grow. It has to unfold. You give it the belief which gives it the space in which to unfold. Nothing can manifest without space. Your belief system is the space of the unfoldment of that particular idea or flower bud. You say, "I believe in it; I am moving it as best I can; I trust and accept that it can be," thus you give it the space to grow through its normal stages.

Suppose you meet somebody you like, and you want to see that person more. You trust that this person would also like to see you. You are asking for and creating the possibility of seeing each other again. Your trust is creating a space in which your friendship can grow. The friendship is creating a space in which a love can grow. Love is creating a space in which all things can grow. Love is the most powerful energy in the universe. The process is one of movement toward, acceptance of, and the readiness and willingness to accept that it can be. From the acceptance and the participation comes the fulfillment. There is nothing on earth that you learn, there is nothing on earth that you achieve that does not go through the process. The process is a need which becomes a desire, from desire comes a participation, and from the participation comes a fulfillment.

You have a need to serve and the need to be respected for those services. The desire to make it happen puts it in action. That participation brings the manifestation from which the fulfillment can come. That is why half-cocked ideas and wishy-washy thought patterns never materialize or manifest. You are not really desiring it; you are only mouthing it.

If your focus is on having your own home, you have to believe that it is all right for you to have a home. Recognize that the home you can afford right now will be based on what you earn. That is all part of the package. You have parallel roads. You must choose whether to wait and use the present time to escalate your money or accept the house you can afford and use that as a stepping stone to a future home.

Whatever you might decide, it has to be positive. Listen to the words you used as you focused on your choice. If you are using words like "everything is blocking me," you are blocking yourself. Can you see what often happens? *You have to think it can happen and be willing to accept it.* Ask that the right and perfect house be shown to you. The parallel route might be to wait another year and build a larger bank balance. Let *that* be the sole focus of your money, which means you may have to sacrifice some other thing. You must be willing to put your full energy into your decision and not look back.

It is very important to be aware of how you are thinking about anything you want to bring into your life. Your thought patterns, if they are negative or restricting, will work against you and will block you. Many people are discouraged because it does not happen instantly. If you believe enough in it, you will stay with it. The moment you start declaring it is being denied you, you set in motion the pattern of denial to you.

People do not realize that the words they use are setting up a pattern for the rest of their lives. It is important to realize that thought and action affect not only one area of life but *all* areas of life. A negative attitude at home affects what happens in the office.

Many times someone puts a lot of work into bringing about a change for the better in their life; and when that change arrives, they feel overwhelmed by it all. For some, the good they have worked for becomes a painful thing. Do not think of achieving as suffering. There is no suffering in achievement. Achievement may demand hard work, but it is not suffering. Lying in a hospital bed in pain is suffering. Sometimes everything seems to happen at once, and the responsibility of it is a little frightening. Recognize that a little fright never hurt anyone. Accept that it is not a failure to feel frightened. Instead take it one day at a time and work through the adjustments that will make it possible for you to be comfortable. Take one day at a time and tell yourself, "There's nothing in this day that I don't have the ability to take care of."

If you do not accomplish some of the things that were presented to you, it is simply a matter of saying thank you for the ability to handle all that I did. Tomorrow I'll finish the rest. The thing that you have to realize is that there are only so many hours in the day and so much accomplishment that can occur. If you have accomplished even half of what is there, you are doing a good job. Look to that which you have accomplished and not that which was left unfinished. Otherwise you are looking at a negative instead of a positive. Know that you have the ability and can finish what is left tomorrow.

Think of something you would like to manifest in your life. Focus on one objective. Next ask yourself what you see or feel is blocking you from it. Ask yourself how achieving that will affect the other aspects of your life—your family, your friends, your children, your lover. The next question to ask yourself is whether there is any association between the effect on them and what you saw as a blockage? The last question to ask yourself is whether you are being *honest* about that comparison.

The formula is:

1. Decide on a *single* goal you wish to achieve.
2. Identify the blockages you feel are there.
3. How will achieving the goal affect others?

4. Is there an association between the effect on others and what you see as a blockage?
5. Are you being honest about the comparison?

Your full discovery pattern might go something like this: Let us suppose that you would like to further your education. You may have a family, a spouse, or a companion to support. If you go to school full time, how are you going to support that schooling and the family obligations? Can your bank account manage it? If you go to school part time and work, can you manage that? There are only x number of hours in a day, will this allow you some time with your family? Realize that your decisions affect everyone around you. Check to see if they are realistic for you and your energy as well. If you go to school part time, it is going to take you longer to achieve your goal, but if it fits the pattern of the rest of your life better, it then serves you best. There might be other ways as well. Perhaps an affluent relative might want to help you. Examine even that. What kind of string is attached to that money? Is it a loan, which you then have to pay back? Is it a gift that you still have to pay back in some form? How does that affect you and your family? You have to look at all the ramifications of each of the steps. When you really look at the ramifications of each step, you may decide you don't want it. It is only by looking at the *full* package that you will really know what is best for you.

Sometimes you have not been facing the fact that there are others involved in your decision. By looking at those who might be affected by your decision, you will clarify it for yourself. You will really see how *you* have been thinking about it. In that way, you begin to bring clarity to the situation so that you can move forward and accomplish more.

If you do not have obligations to others, you then go through the same process in relationship to yourself. What do you feel is blocking you? How many alternate routes are there to help you circumvent them? For instance, many times a shortage of money is seen as a blockage. Ask yourself if it really is? Are you willing to do some extra work for a while to gain extra cash? Have you investigated thoroughly if financial help is available, or have you only listened to other people's opinions on it? Do you want the goal enough to earn it? The object of this exercise is threefold. One, it helps you decide whether you really want it; two, it helps you face your *own self-created* blockages; and three, it brings clarity that helps you find other ways of approaching the situation.

If your blockage is not a blockage that comes from some other source but comes from within yourself, then, literally, the first person who has to recognize it is *you.* If you do not think you are good enough, then nobody else can. If you do not think you are worthy of respect, how can anybody else respect you? You have to say, "I m worthy of recognition, and I shall have it through my effort in my right and perfect time." Recognition must come from within you.

Working with this exercise on something you are trying to achieve in your life is the first step toward feeling good about yourself. It will develop self-esteem. In having gone through the process of sorting it out, you start to feel more secure about it because there are no hidden factors. You have through it through, therefore, have taken away the fear that there is only one way to achieve it. *You have also been honest with your - self.* It is important to respect yourself enough to be honest with yourself. That is a miracle, and it is wonderful. You must respect what you do, for that is truly achieving. If you feel you are not worthy of that respect, attack the space you feel unworthy in and change it.

The person who goes around saying they are ugly eventually grows warts. If you feel ugly, ask yourself what it is you think is ugly. Is your hair a mess? Fix it. Do you need a shave? Fix it. Whatever you need to fix, fix it. Instead of complaining, do something.

If you have continual conflict within and vacillate, you will have to ask yourself why you are using vacillation as an escape route from facing a potential or a desire. Many times a person will have a desire and because, for some reason, they think they are not worthy of it, or cannot have it, they vacillate. They say, "This is what I want—no, that is what I want." You have to ask yourself why you can not have both? It is as simple as that. There is no reason why you cannot have both. Go after one, and when you have achieved that, go after the other.

You can, of course, continue to say you do not know what you want, and that is exactly where you will be all your life. When there is a choice to make, you make the choice; and once you have made it, you put all your energy into that choice. Do not worry whether you make the right choice. If you do that, you are going back to wanting both of them. You say, "This is what I choose to do in this point in time." Go for it, put all your energy into it. When you achieve it, you will have the full potential of self-esteem, fulfillment, and satisfaction. At that point, if you feel you want to go after the other, go for it. You will not leave yourself sitting on a fence and going nowhere if you make a decision. If you are not willing to make a decision, fate will make the decision for you.

AFFIRMATION FOR SELF-ESTEEM

The following affirmation consists of twelve powerful statements. You will work with them for twelve days in the following manner:

PHASE I

First day: Use the first statement once every hour for twelve hours. (You may affirm it aloud or silently.) Really listen to the statement as you affirm it.

In the evening, before you retire, read the entire affirmation (all twelve statements) once.

Second day: Use the second statement and follow the same procedure you did with statement one. Again, in the evening before bedtime, read the complete affirmation.

Proceed each day with the next statement until all twelve statements have been used.

PHASE II

Next read the complete affirmation twice a day for twelve weeks. It would be best to read it on arising and at bedtime. However, you may find other times more convenient and that is acceptable too. The object is to affirm in the morning and in the evening.

If you follow this exercise through, you will be amazed at how differently you feel about you and about your world.

AFFIRMATION FOR SELF-ESTEEM

Within me is potential and the power to make it move.
I accept that potential.

Within me is the power to shape and mold my life.
Through mental Direction, I shape and mold.

I accept that ability and power will direct my life.
I make clear decisions without fear.

In Creative Force is the raw essence of every idea.
Through my mind, I tap that pure essence.

My intellect merges with raw idea.
I bring forth new concepts.

I trust new venture and direction.
I release old blockages and fear.

The spirit and power of thought are manifest in me.
My thoughts are powerful and pure.

I permit those thoughts to shape my life.
I rejoice in my positive direction of it.

I fear not, I am empowered to create my perfect space.
Through divine potential, I move forward.

Empowerment fulfills me by my proper action
I wisely choose those actions.

My space is wholeness on every level.
My movement is toward my good.

I am renewed in thought—
     empowered to act—
          and ready to achieve.

       THIS IS MY TRUTH.

             So be it.

Change is actually intuitive thought put in motion with respect..

CHAPTER III

PREPARATION FOR SELF-RELIANCE

Let us look at those qualities which assist you in developing a sense of self-reliance. It is important to see where you have been, analyze where you are, and question where you want to go.

The person you have become (up to this point in your life) has developed over the years. You have been shaped and molded by your own inner potential interacting with situations, people, and places. In the early years of life, you are influenced greatly by others. Your parents began that shaping by guiding you through those early years. Later schooling and friends add to the process. All of this is seen and used by you *through your own interpretation and understanding*. How you *react* also builds who you become.

Evolution means movement. To evolve, you must be willing to change and alter the past in you. Bending means building. Rigidity can lock you into a point in time through idea, attitude, or refusal to permit change. As you build toward self-reliance, you will be examining the you that has developed over the years. You will be asking questions of yourself and may feel a little timid about some of the answers you get. You may not like all the answers, but trust them. They will be helping you find the real you.

Interaction with others is a chance to grow. Each of you are seeking growth through balance, therefore, you learn from each other's experiences. Interaction may, at times, not be pleasant, but even conflict—if you let it—can help you see yourself and learn from others.

You have been brought up to accept humbleness; you have been brought up to believe that to give is more blessed than to receive. Where does one draw the line that keeps us from taking away the joy of giving for someone else? He who never lets another help them has taken away the joy of giving, he has taken away the ability for that person to share. We are looking for the balance between the two. In this chapter and those that follow, we will be working on preparation for self-reliance, preparation for knowing that you *can* rely on yourself and still receive assistance from others. You do not have to give up all outside support, but you have to know that you are self-reliant. If you are so independent that you see assistance as a weakness, you may be afraid of appearing less or afraid of sharing.

Let us first consider the word "self." If you are saying "me," "I," or "self," you are really talking about three aspects of yourself—mind, body, and soul. You can become *mentally* prepared for life and not be prepared in the *soul* nor in the body. In other words, you can become so one-tracked in your consideration of *self* that you forget the rest of you. Thus you must bring balance to all of those parts of you. Know with a certainty that in addition to the seriousness of yourself, you must also know the humor of yourself. You must know that thought is the projector, but to complete the cycle, it must be part of your physical action and your spiritual understanding. Lovely thoughts must go further than lovely thoughts. Have you ever stopped and thought to yourself, "I know I can do that. I can write a better book than that any day—I can paint a better picture than that any day. I can do that," and thoroughly convinced mentally that you can, you leave it alone. It is much easier, is it not? If you truly accepted it, you would be willing to step out and do it—in some form. You do not necessarily have to paint the same kind of picture, or write the same kind of book, but you could put your thoughts in writing, and you could put your color and form into some kind of creative endeavor. Then you have learned a lesson of truly understanding that particular thing. *Now* you *really* know that you can do it.

You may have read a lot of books about baking bread, and you may have a lot of recipes; but until you bake a loaf, you never know the joy of pounding, kneading, letting the frustrations out, and the delightful smell of it when it is baking. You have not truly experienced it in body and soul until you take the action to make it so. The first place you begin to learn to trust yourself is in following through. As you read this material, I suggest you follow through on some small thoughts in preparation for following through on larger thoughts later on. He who claims he can write the better book, until he struggles with putting it on paper, does not know or appreciate the author of *any* book. In taking into yourself an understanding of what writing means, you have given the gift of appreciation to the author and yourself. It does not matter if it is a painter, a hair stylist, or a plummer. This breaks down barriers of non-communication and a lack of understanding of where other people are coming from. It gives you an understanding of their skill, potential, or beauty. The casual statement that says, "I can," has to be taken further. That is learning to truly understand yourself through what another does. Through the accomplishment of somebody else, you come into the understanding of the ability to accomplish something yourself.

If you try something and you find it is harder than you thought, you then have another decision to make. Do I pass the nearest waste basket and drop it, or do I permit myself to acquire some new knowledge pertaining to it? If you are truly going to know yourself, you are going to understand that there are some things you do *not* do as well as others. Think how boring life would be without an exchange in any manner because everybody did it all. Learn from the experience of discovering that you do not have to *know* it all, and you do not have to *do* it all. There are those who teach, and there are those who listen, but the teacher is worthless without those who listen. The artist has no fulfillment if there is no one to appreciate his painting. You are not less because you might not do it as well as someone else. Therein lies the experience of self-realization.

In the present evolutionary vibration, new things will

occur. Some will be temporary, and some will last. When you get a spontaneous idea, do not be afraid to voice it, do not be afraid to bring it to fruition. Do not say that that is dumb; they never needed it before, why would they need it now. It is a time of spontaneity within the self, a time of releasing these small gems that surprise you as well as everyone else. If you will permit that to happen, you will be coming to still another realization of yourself. If these sparks of creative force are ignored, nothing will come to fruition.

Spontaneous action and thoughts are of a creative bent; and when you permit something spontaneous to occur, you have released the creative force from within. There was a time in your world when all flowers lived in the ground. Now they live in hanging pots of various shapes and forms, according to the spontaneous expression of the potter; and, in turn, the spontaneous need of an individual who sees one and brings it home. Each time a new and innovative idea is brought to fruition, it is answering the energy of the time period it is being experienced in. Look at the shapes and forms in your world today. They are not round and square and triangular; they are free form, they are many-sided. It is all new expressions of old energies. Everything that exists must come to a new expression in a new Age, so *you* will be the spontaneous bearers of new concepts. *Your* job will be to let it out. When you get the idea that seems very humorous, do not be afraid to follow through. You will have done two things. You will have given somebody a laugh, and you will feel fulfilled

If any of you have something that you have stored away and not looked at for a long time, think about it, then take it out and look at it. You will be amazed at how wrong your concept of what it looked like was. it will be smaller or larger than you thought, or a slightly different shade of color than you thought. As you disassociate with something, your concept of it begins to fade. Have you ever noticed that if you try to return to a place of your childhood, it is not half as large as you thought it was? You are larger than you were then, but the concept of it is retained from the point you first understood it. When you go back to it in another time, it is different.

If you have many things stored, I would suggest that you take them out and look at them. You will find that some of them no longer have a relationship to you at all, but may fit another need at this time. You can let go of some things and retain others. What are you doing? You are building a non-reliance on material things. Now this does not mean that a material thing is not good. It does not mean that it has not served you or that other material things will not serve you in the future. It is the understanding that the *only* thing that is absolute is change, that *you* are changing, and that your *needs* are changing. The vibration you live in is changing, therefore, some material things will no longer serve you in the same manner at this point in time. Find a different use for them or release them.

Every human being is, at times, sentimental. How many of you have every picture your child ever drew from the time he or she was able to hold a pencil? Everyone of those experiences are in the mind and the heart. They do not have to be there in the material form. They can be released. Any experience that you have had, that you feel close to, lives with you and in you. There are some things that you can let go of and still retain the joy. There are other things you may want to hold on to because you are not quite ready to let go of them, and that is quite all right. Do not approach self-reliance like a bull-dozer. You are to approach it as an understanding. You are not suppose to throw anything away until you *understand that you no longer need it.* One holds on to something because they are not finished with them. The one thing that can become a trap is holding on to something sentimentally so strongly that you expect it to always be the same. Heaven help us if your children still see you as they did at the age of four. I am sure you would not find the child's self-drawn card holding the same joy if done when the child is forty-two.

During the process of evolution within, you are dealing with the changing vibratory rate of yourself and others. As you begin to understand your own energies, you begin to use them as a tool to help you in life. You sometimes call them hunches. For instance, if you do not feel comfortable, there is something that is not in exact synchronization with your vibration. Go inward and find out what it is in you that is out of accord with the situation. What inside you is not comfortable? You will then discover what expectations you had, mentally or physical-ly that you do not quite feel are being answered. Accept that while you are uneasy at the moment, that can change. Being out of synchronization with the situation is perfectly all right.

The thing to remember is that you are a unique individual and that individuality has to be permitted to exist. You are not here to be sheep; you are not here to agree with everybody in thought, idea, and emotion. There will be exchanges of ideas and opinions about issues. You listen to them with the under-standing that you must then address them with your own uniqueness. You have the divine right to accept or reject the theory. It is important that your uniqueness be open to concepts which you then take, mentalize, and internalize. Through your own focus and direction, you take that which is acceptable to you and begin to put it into motion in your life.

Feeling out of synchronization can be a signal for adjustment, not necessarily abandonment. When you try something new, meet new people, or change jobs, there is a period of adjustment that occurs during which time you may feel ill at ease. Sometimes that can occur with something as simple as a color or new style. Suppose you have always lived in a very relaxed style—jeans, sweatshirts, cut-offs, etc. Then comes an occasion where suit and tie or heels and dress are called for. You may find yourself ill at ease until you begin to relax enough to accept that you look pretty darn good! The awkwardness leaves because you gave it a chance. It is good policy to keep tabs on whether or not your letting casual become slob. Like yourself enough to dress up occasionally just for *you*. By differentiating between uneasy and bad, by taking time to look inward and adjust, you keep yourself from getting in a rut and from missing exciting new things.

Self-reliance means trust. Who are you trusting? Yourself. I would say that the one that is *least* trusted at any time is the *self*. Other people's opinions help you make decisions, but the finalization of any act in your life must be based on *your* ability to trust yourself. If you trust yourself, you are going to take the internalization of that thing, act upon it, and materialize it in your life. If you meet someone self-assured who seems to have a direction in life, there is a tendency to go one of two ways. You could feel very comfortable with them because they make you feel secure, or you could feel the need to run from

them as fast as you can because they make you feel so insecure. You must realize that anything that they are, you can be if
you *choose* to translate it through your *own* uniqueness. If
every creative person painted the same picture, it would be
very dull. However, some are potters, some are painters, some
are writers, some are gourmet cooks, some sew beautifully,
and others crochet. There are ten million other paths that go
along with a creative venture, but they are all the uniqueness
of the individual translating the same energy creatively.

When you come across people who feel secure in themselves, accept that they have gotten to that point by working
within themselves. You must not see that as a threat, and you
must not see that as your goal, but see it as someone who has
"gotten it together." Do not be the puppet, do not be the mime,
be the unique individual seeking that potential in *yourself* and
developing it.

To be self-reliant in large things, you must be self-reliant in
small things. If you cannot feel good about yourself in small
ways, you are not going to be able to support the larger things.
You begin by doing well things that are very normal everyday
things. If you have a home, have a home that is, to the best of
your ability, warm and open. It is a home that is tidy. Tidy does
not mean scrubbing the walls daily, but it does mean cleaning
the crumbs off the kitchen floor. You cannot blame a home for
not being a nice home if you have not treated it nicely. That is
a very common everyday example. You do not think of it as a
spiritual thing, but it is, because *your home is an expression of
you and how you feel about your place of dwelling and your -
self.* Your body is home for the spirit and soul to dwell in. You
must also think in terms of caring for that physical being. You

have to understand that it all relates to you. It does not matter if your home is a single room, a huge dwelling, or a mobile home. It does not matter. What matters is that *its condition is a reflection of how you feel about yourself.* Take time to put a single flower in a paper cup, if necessary, to bring joy and beauty into your small place. Take time to wash the windows so the sunlight can shine in. These are things that make you self-reliant on a very physical, mundane level, but it is the beginning of being self-reliant in other areas.

Self-reliance is not only trusting yourself but also accepting your accomplishments. Most people are very embarrassed if someone gives them praise. Have you ever received compliments and felt almost embarrassed? The object is this: When you are given a compliment, simply say thank you. You do not have to be ashamed because you have done something very well.

If physical acts express you, mental acts are also expressing you. If you were to have a thought about a person sitting next to you, according to that thought, the person would either begin to feel like moving their seat, or they might want to move a little closer. It is a *mental* action, the mind projecting. Have you ever entered a place and felt rejected? Nobody smiled, nobody said welcome. You begin to assume people are thinking negative things about you. Why? Why do you assume that you must be unwelcome? Maybe *you* do not think you are worthy of welcome.

Do not depend upon another's opinion or emotion to make you a worthy being. This does not prevent you from getting help from each other, and it does not mean that another cannot share an opinion with you or that you cannot ask another's opinion. Understand that if their opinion is not the same as yours, you do not have to immediately assume you have conflict. Accept that that may happen. Do not ask for an opinion if you are only asking in order to be agreed with. Be confident in your own opinion and be open to another's view.

Self-reliance rests on the combined level of your physical, mental, and spiritual being. It can never rest on one of these qualities alone. Many of you say you will rely on the God in you and let all else occur. You can rely on God in you, and He can give you the nudge, the incentive, and the intuition; but if you do not get up and start making a movement in the physical self, it cannot happen. You are His manifestation in this world; therefore, you are the one who puts it into action in this world. He can show you how, but you have to live it.

Every time there is that feeling of being insecure or unsure, it is important for you to be still and listen to get that inner guidance. The inner influence gives you the opportunity to let your uniqueness speak to you. When that happens, you must use the direction it gives you in some manner.

More and more in this new age energy frequency, people run around in circles; and in running in circles, they create nothing. It is a big zero. You must permit the energy to *focus in some direction* so it can be used. When you are dealing with building self-reliance, you must first break away from outer reliance. You must sometimes withdraw into yourself to get perspective. Sometimes when there is anger in the self, or a non-acceptance within the self of something that is occurring in life, there will be a tendency to deliberately do something that is self-destructive. What you are really doing is seeking an excuse for your own unhappiness. Some people will turn to alcohol, some to drugs, and some to other roads or forms of self-degradation. They really do not want to accept themselves, or a weakness within themselves. They try to make the weakness a strength, and by doing that, they are running away from themselves. Temper tantrums are an escape route. Self-pity is an escape route. Substances are an escape route. Stop running and face the issue, and you will be amazed at how strong and self-reliant you can be.

"They." There is an amazing group of people called "they." "*They* don't let me do it." "*They* cause all the problems in my life." There is another marvelous group called "everybody." "*Everybody* does it." "*Everybody* says it is so." If you were asked to name two, you could not. The object is that you are *purposely* putting what *you are mad about in yourself* outside of yourself. When you do not want to be responsible, you take a route that leads you to being irresponsible. If you are not willing to take a chance on yourself, you will become vulnerable to taking a chance on everything. If you are not willing to accept a vulnerability in yourself, you will take a route that will make you vulnerable to others. Recognize that when you frequently try to place responsibility for your actions outside yourself, you are expressing the fear of being self-reliant.

Society is expressing anger and moving away from the discipline that *it* has created as a culture. It is creating fantasy heroes and all of them are outside the self. The good guy drives the fastest car and does the most tricks. The super-hero puts on the cloak in the phone booth and saves everybody.

Where in this is there anything which is telling you to rely upon yourself. Man, more and more, chooses not to look inward, but wants direction to come from others. If that doesn't happen, he often begins to use fantasy as a way of removing himself from the reality of the situation. The super-hero now becomes the huge UFO which will save him. Fantasy has its place. It can teach and amuse, but it is not meant to replace self-reliance. Reliance has to start with self. If you are going to be a super-hero, let it be to yourself first.

You need to recognize that it takes only one attempt at self-reliance to plant the seed. A new beginning comes from a single seed. One single overcoming, one single facing of that which you have refused to face before, or chosen not to overcome before, puts the thing in motion. Then all you have to do is nurture it. When you turn away from a negative habit, you begin to move toward greater self-reliance. If you can make yourself take the other road just once, every time you are tempted again, you will think of the success of the last time. Focus on the positive, and it will take you forward to a more positive direction.

When you take a destructive route in any way, you are demanding that *somebody else* tell you to stop. You are demanding inwardly that somebody else become your self-reliance and tell you not to do it. Did you ever notice how smug you feel when you have crossed against the light and made it? "Ah-hah! I beat the odds." If you look at these very little ways in which you express those inner things, you will begin to understand more and more that you do express needs and desires.

Have you ever heard people say they are on vacation, and, therefore, they don't have to do this and don't have to do that? Moving away from doing what they did as a regular routine removed the feeling that they *had to do*. Recognize that you have to get up, you have to eat, you have to go to work, and you have to... But on vacation, you do not *have* to. A vacation permits a person to move away from what they did as a regular routine. This helps them to keep the balance between a fixed routine and a relaxed expression of themselves. It must also be realized that if their routine leaves them feeling dominated by what they *have to do*, they need to take another look at it. Perhaps they need to see that what a job calls for is not a punishment, but rather the job's need. Perhaps too much power is being given to the words " have to."

Very often, there is a tendency for people to immediately resent anything that has a "have to" associated with their endeavors, even though it is their choice. People cannot wait to buy a home, and then they immediately talk about *having* to mow the lawn, *having* to pay the rent. That was all part of the package when they took it, but now they see it as something that is separating them from the thing they originally wanted. You have to ask yourself how much you are willing to give for what you get. You have to understand that that is all a part of your own decision. Suppose you say you like the outdoors and, therefore, want a whole wall of windows. Do you like to wash windows? Maybe that had better be a consideration, because you are going to rely on yourself for cleaning the windows when you have that house. You are going to rely on you any time the "chips are down."

You are going to rely on you any time a decision has to be

made that is going to be meaningful. No matter how many other people give you opinions, in the end, *you* have to make the decision. One of the first steps toward self-reliance is the recognition that the responsibility for what returns is yours. *I can have a temper tantrum. I probably will not be invited back again, but I can have the momentary joy of that temper tantrum.* If you do not look beyond that moment, you could find yourself with less than you had in the beginning.

Any time you are making a decision about yourself, you have to know that you are going to be relying on you. The return from the decision is of your making. There will be nobody else coming in and taking care of it. When you feel that you are ready to take the responsibility and be self-reliant in decision making, it does not matter whether anybody else thinks you should have or not. It is yours—yours to work with, yours to do with as you will. The only reliance that you can truly depend on at any time is self-reliance. The ability for that self-reliance comes from the God-Self within. In you there is security, safety, direction, and all that is needed.

It is generally recognized that collective effort is the most successful effort. This is true provided that the collective effort is a collection of *already proven* efforts. What is meant by this is that if people are self-reliant and secure in themselves, they are better able to interact, integrate, and make a collective effort more successful. The most important thing, whether your effort is collective or singular, is to know the self and to know what you have to rely on.

This chapter will approach several areas of breaking down the blockages to self-reliance. It will start by breaking down your own comprehension of weaknesses and strengths within you. I am then going to help you to come to grips with the vague and shadowy places that you fear within yourself.

First realize that the word "acceptance" is very important in working with self-reliance. The word "acceptance" means accepting your *abilities* and your *non-abilities*. Does that seem strange when we are talking about positive thinking? When we talk of accepting your non-abilities, we are not talking about a negative. We are talking about the recognition that one is often stronger in one ability than in another.

The word "success" conjures up many things, material things, as well as spiritual and emotional things. It can be that to some success means security—the security of a loved one, the security of an income, or the security of a place to be and food to eat. They are all part of the security pattern. However, not everybody needs the same thing to feel secure. Very often, in the teachings of a spiritual nature, the impression is given that material things can be very destructive. They can only be a negative influence if they are being permitted to *own you* instead of *you owning them*. Recognize that there will be a time in your life when things will be important to you and a time when they will not. Everyone goes through phases of needing greater exterior security and then needing less of that sort of security as they move through life. There is nothing to say that, later on, you might not decide you need things again, but it is how you need them that determines *how* self-reliant you are.

Here is a simple method for breaking old molds and old patterns. Take a piece of clothing out of the closet that you do *not* like and wear it, because in the wearing of it, you will come to the realization that the clothes are not you, *you* are the clothes. It is breaking down the acceptance that an external thing is making you. Everybody has things they feel comfortable in, and everybody has things they feel a little less comfortable in. Everybody has "the lucky shirt." Something good happened while you were wearing it, and so you feel that every time you wear it, something good is going to happen. What you must learn is that *you* are the lucky shirt and *you* are the uncomfortable garment, that you make or break it by how you feel about yourself *inside*.

You decide—all along the way—what your reality is. Many times people have raved about a certain thing when they neither understood it, liked it, or cared about it, because it was the "in thing." Television commercials tell you about all the magical things that will happen when you use their products. Fashion trends dictate skirt lengths, styles and colors, and the width of ties and lapels. If you buy the package without question, you are letting yourself be ruled by outside influences. If you compare it to your *inner* feelings about life, you may find that you don't feel comfortable about them.

People adorn themselves ridiculously because it is the "in thing," whether it is becoming to them or not. Don't fall into the trap. Think about it, then *you* choose.

There are all kinds of fantasies promulgated in your world. In your world, there is a tendency to create fantasies about people. They are labeled as groups instead of seen as individuals. For instance, the general attitude is that every large, tall man is *expected* to be rugged. Every man of slight build is expected *not* to be. How ridiculous! Do blondes have more fun? It seems to me that there are a lot of brunettes and redheads who are very happy in your world. People begin to accept things, not as incidentals in life, but as dyed-in-the-wool facts. They begin to accept them and live them. A short person may feel that not being tall is a fault. Rather than develop all the wonderful qualities they do have, they concentrate on what they see as a lack. They can bemoan their height all their lives or become aggressive and belligerent to prove how big they are. Meanwhile, the tall person is beginning to slouch because they feel too tall. What a waste of who they really are!

Think for a moment of what you consider or fear within yourself as a blockage. What do you see in yourself as a detriment to you in your life? If you are lucky, you will have to think very hard. That means you do not have it on the surface. Everybody has something they feel in some way blocks them in life. Some have it right up on the surface where they face it every day, and some have it pushed way down inside them where it only sneaks up periodically and shocks them. Once you know it is there, then you have to ask yourself where it came from. Search out its birthing place. Are you afraid to walk under a ladder or see a black cat? Where did it come from? Those are very surface incidents, what you call superstitions, but they represent fears. Now ask yourself what you have done to overcome it? "What have I done to defuse it, to take its power away? Do I want to?" Does that sound strange—do I want to? Does having that blockage, that fear, give you an escape route? Has it become something you cherish in your life? Is it the thing that lets you say, "Okay, I know I can't do that because...?" Ask yourself what you have done to change it.

Realize that as you look for a blockage, it is not meant to be done negatively. It is meant to be a comprehension and an acceptance. If you have something you feel is a blockage, do not see it as making you a lesser being. Do not see it as a deterrent. See it as a part of your reality that you are perfectly able to control. Through the comprehension of it and the understanding of it, you take away its power and you are able, then, to alter and change it.

There is no job that cannot be right and perfect for you if you will accept the proper amount of *responsibility* to it. You also need to recognize when to draw the line. You need to know when you have gone beyond your ability *of the moment*. Trying to do what you are not *yet* capable of can be very frustrating. When you reach that state, pause and decide how to handle it. Learn the next step and then proceed or if that isn't feasible right then, seek assistance. Know that everybody is not a painter, everybody is not an author, everybody is not good at math, and everybody is not bilingual. I could go on for hours telling you what everybody is not, but for all the "is nots," there are some who *are*. Knowing what your special qualities are and using that potential brings you happiness. You cannot be everything; you are not meant to be everything. You are meant to know yourself. You are meant to permit that self to unfold and bloom to the best possible potential that you have.

Have you ever gone to a gathering where everybody had been to a play or movie except you? How did you feel? Probably left out, or maybe even a bit uninformed. There is a tendency to see a non-participation as something that is a failing in you. It is not. There is nothing to say that you will not see that show at some other time. You might have thought that particular performance would be boring. There are some who enjoy museums, and there are some who hate them because they are not in their particular interest. There is nothing wrong with having that attitude just as there is no reason to feel guilty because someone says museums are great. You have to watch yourself; and when you feel the insecurities creeping in right then and there, ask yourself why.

Everyone has varying degrees of education, varying degrees of travel, and varying degrees of experiences; but in sharing them, everybody is enriched. The next time somebody tells you they have just come back from wherever, say, "That's nice, tell me about it. I've never been there."

If you have come to accept that you feel a blockage, you have taken the first step in breaking it, for you cannot end something that you do not know exists. It may be a blockage in relationships, in business areas, or financial returns. It may be that you felt that the blockage had to do with dis-ease in the body. Finally, it may even be that you feel a blockage that has to do with spiritual growth. The point I want to make is that you usually feel it has an association with a specific area in your life.

I want you to ask yourself three questions. Think about them.
1. Why do I see this as a problem?
2. How much does this influence my life?

Think about it. Is it something that happens once in a while? Is it something that is an underlying thing all the time? How often does this affect you?

3. To what end do I think I would go to change it?

How far are you willing to go to change it? That may seem like a strange question, but when you present it to yourself in silence, you are going to find several reactions. One may be: Let's stop this process because I do not really want to attempt change. Another may be: I cannot. I want to go all the way, but I can't because...! You may find yourself listing more and more reasons why any avenue of change won't work. That is all right, it is quite normal. That begins to show you a pattern. You don't have to fear this exercise. You are doing it with *you*, no one else. When you start counting all the reasons why you can't make something work, you are usually afraid that if you try, it *won't* work.

After you have answered those questions, there is another questions I want you to ask:

4. If this is my failing, or my weak spot, or my fear, or my blockage, then what is my strength?

First you are going to investigate why you see this as a blockage, how often it affects you, and how far you are willing to go to change it. Ask yourself: If this is your blockage, what is the thing that opens the gate for you. By the Universal Law of Polarity, every weakness has its opposite. By recognizing this, you are able to accept the strengths within yourself which bring balance.

Recognize that anything you do in your life must be from the heart and your true desire. It cannot be competitive, nor can it be of the "I'll show them" attitude. When you try to accomplish in order to prove something to someone else, you will be doing it for the wrong reason. Do it for *you*. Doing it for the wrong reasons, invariably, will not bring happiness. You have to know it is yours because *you want it*. You must want it because it is yours, not because you are going to prove something to someone, show somebody something, or get even with somebody.

In the competitive fields of business, one expects competition. It does not have to be brought into your life to the degree that your entire life becomes competitive. You can handle interaction in the competitive field, but let it come from your heart and your spirit. There is no place that gives a better chance to prove your spirituality than the business world, because it is a friction world. Focus your life with the realization that you can interact in a very busy field and still hold your own.

One of the things that you must understand when you are working in a competitive field is that competition is part of the game. The game plan for yourself must include the realization that this is so, and you must not personalize it in the sense that it is against you alone. When you are in a direct competition, there will be those who are vying against you for the bid, for the job, for whatever, and that is a direct energy exchange, but it is only because the game plan calls for competition. It is not because someone is out to get you. You have to permit personal detachment enough to handle the competition without fear of failure. Recognize that while competition is there, it is part of life.

One must never refute what they have while trying to have more, for it is like trying to build a house with no foundation.

Every bit of gain, whether it is experience, money, or new comprehension within a field, must be looked upon as an asset. They must be looked upon as something to help you rather than something that is not enough. When you are working in a financial realm and your objective is financial gain, you must see that you are gaining in some way all along the way, because if you do not, you are going to block it. You are going to close the door to more. You must also ask yourself how you are handling gain. In any working situation, there is more to it than the money. There is the self-esteem factor, there is the power factor, there are many different factors that come into play in that financial structure. You have to know the whole of why you are doing something in order to totally understand it. If you say you wish to gain and you believe you are, you will achieve it. However, if you are approaching it with lack of self-belief, you will not because you have already said you are not worthy. You have already set the goal that says you cannot make it. You have to be willing to gain the potential, work with the potential, accept the potential, and move forward with it. Then you are not closing the door on what can come to you.

You cannot half-heartedly participate in something in the competitive field. If you say from nine to five I do this job and I get this check, then nine to five belongs to that job by your *own* decision in the acceptance of the wage. There is a responsibility to the job as well as to yourself, and you cannot cheat on one hand and expect to gain on the other. Bring balance and harmony to the package you are working with. You must also value yourself enough to put a value on your work. All true work effort expended has a right to recompense. You can be as altruistic as you want where finances are concerned, but be altruistic to the degree that you are willing to accept that it is going to affect the total financial package. In other words, honor your contract and yourself.

In developing self-reliance, you must overcome fear. when you have a fear, you have to isolate it and see it for what it is. You then have to ask yourself how much power you are going to give it. In other words, if you fear that you are going to be mugged on the street, you can get yourself so fearful that you send out signals that say, "Here I am, I'm vulnerable." Instead, take all the precautions you can and don't walk in dark alleys in the wee hours of the morning. You can then say to yourself, "If I'm taking all those precautions, I know that I will not send out the wrong signals." Take the physical, logical steps that give you a new attitude. When you have done that, you will know that you have taken care of it. The thought pattern creates change. What you think, you attract.

Remember that fear is very often used as a tool to escape involvement. When fear of anything occupies the thoughts constantly, it blocks the ability to think constructively. If one fears enough, he immobilizes himself. One must replace the fear with action that brings you in touch with life. You will soon find the *excitement of the doing* will out-weigh the fear. If you find yourself with a great fear of letting go, try to relax and surrender to your higher self.

Fear leaves you vulnerable. it leaves you frightened of change and vulnerable to all the side fears as well, those that lay hidden in you. You can be leery of not being in control and, therefore, fear the outcome of a situation. It is not easy to let go. Again you ask the questions: What difference would it make, what difference would it make if the horse went to the left instead of to the right? You must inspire yourself to take a chance. The objective being, if you can let go in a small way, you will gradually bring into the life the ability to let go in a larger way.

Accept that it is going to be all right and that *the fear* is not the thing with the power. The fear has only the power *you* give it. Recognizing that you are afraid lets you understand that something needs correction. If you don't take a moment to find out what it is you are really afraid of, you begin to promulgate and project fear of everything. Pinpoint it and start working on what can alter it, and you won't be building and strengthening fearful attitudes in yourself. Fear can be given so much power by you that it actually manifests. Sometimes a person will fear an illness so much that he or she will actually develop it. Disease is any form of not being at ease within your system. That vibration begins to manifest in physical form.

Sometimes the cure is the acceptance of the presence of the disease. The acceptance does not mean that it becomes a permanent part of you. In accepting that it is all right that you have it, that it is not a failure, that it is not something that you have done wrong, you are able to work with the energy of it and, therefore, give it less power and less ability to manifest. Whenever there is disease, there is a tendency for man to feel that he has failed in some way. You view life as always being perfect. What is perfection? Perfection for one is not perfection for another.

If one person can run up a hill and another cannot, it does not make one person less than the other. The person who cannot run up the hill and tries is a fool, for he has not accepted the fact that, at this point in time, to run up the hill is detrimental to him. He might like to run up the hill, but recognizes he isn't fit. Now if he really wants to take that hill, he will correct within himself whatever needs correcting; and next time he'll take the hill.

Within every handicap, disease, or impediment, there is a growth—a soul growth and a positive thing. By creating a friendship with your disease instead of making an enemy of it, you bring a harmonic to the body which then can begin to alter the cells. Do not fight it; do not give it the power to be your enemy. Accept that it is all right *at this point*. With acceptance, you can begin to alter it. When too much power is given to the handicap, the disease, or the impediment, a battle forms that wears the person out. Making a friend of it instead of a foe, the energy dissipation is not as strong, and it becomes an easier thing to deal with on all levels. Even if you never change the disease, you would change its power over you and the destructive power it has over you. Making a friend of it means accepting that you can work with the body toward change. You won't be bringing further depletion by anger which destroys.

Some people have great difficulty in recognizing within themselves that they are good at what they are doing. When they receive acknowledgement from their boss or their peers they are elated for a few minutes, but then they fall back into that deep abyss of feeling unaccomplished. They are not willing to accept that somebody could approve of what they did. No one can accept you in any phase in your life unless you accept yourself. The acceptance of the beauty of you and the realization that you are not a failure is your key. Know that it is not a tragedy to make a mistake, and it is all right to stumble along the way.

86

Know that it is inner harmony that you are seeking more than outer recognition. That must start in you, and you must take the responsibility for stepping out and making it happen. You must also develop a sense of humor in your thinking patterns to help break down the seriousness. Be able to move away from taking life too seriously. Life is serious, but it is not solemn. It is joyful! Rejoice when you are praised and accept that you have earned it. Earlier we talked about the responsibility that goes with things. If you have honestly earned it, you have the right to the praise, you have the right to the monetary return, and you have the right to anything that goes with it.

Nobody likes to be the loser. Nobody likes to make a mistake. The wonderful thing is that everybody can, everybody does, and everybody will make mistakes; but they do not have to make it a fear. You do have abilities, and you must let them flow. You must trust yourself. The first thing you have to do when you don't feel self-reliant is to recognize that there are many things you do well in life. Let those things flow. For every low point in you, there has to be a high point. See in the everyday things you do the acceptance of and the realization of that joy in you. Understand that it is all right to be you. Your success, your choice of a path, is *yours*. Therefore, it does not have to equal or be the same as someone else's. See and accept your successes each day.

As I have said earlier, if you smile, you are a healer. If you know that you have smiled, you have accepted in yourself the ability to give joy, therefore, you can honor yourself for that, you can see that as something that gives you self-esteem. Self-esteem is the recognition of the qualities of yourself in *all* things you do, not just in a special few. If you tune into the small aspects of you, you will soon find that they build, grow, and become larger. Trust yourself to take chances based on belief in yourself. It does not matter if anybody else sees it as the right way for you; it matters that *you* see it as the right way for you, and accept the responsibility of it.

Many people experience difficulty trying to join their spiritual feelings and their development of spiritual growth with that of their business or commercial reality. Very often they see them as opposites; and, as a result, frustration or conflicts develop which impede the development of growth in either area. When you have more than one area of focus, both areas are going to grow until they merge in one. Spiritual growth is the acceptance that you must play in both ball fields, that each is serving the other. The spiritual unfoldment can help you manifest a more peaceful interaction in the business world. The acceptance that your development is not quite fully achieved yet, prevents you from creating unreal expectations. Prioritize your day, divide it, and let each aspect flow to the degree that is right and perfect for it. Let it rest there until it is ready to become more. Everything that you are using, learning, and gaining in the business world is part of your ability to handle all aspects of spiritual growth. Life is lessons!

Do you think you are not growing spiritually? Is it because you have a checklist that says this week this class, next week that one, and then you'll have it all? Spiritual growth is getting up in the morning, living, breathing, interacting, and growing. In that unfoldment, you permit the energies to escalate, which open to you other things.

It is important to meditate on a daily basis. That creates the harmonic within with the High Self, which permits you to flow in whatever direction your spiritual growth is to be. Your day may be totally business, but the spiritual growth is there. You cannot separate it from anything else in your life. It is not a separate entity. It is a living, breathing, flowing thing, and as you permit that to occur each day, you will find more and more doors opening.

There are no two spiritual beings that ever act the same, and anyone who thinks they can judge the other one has fallen short already. You must let your spiritual essence flow no matter what you are doing, and you must know that some days it will appear as if nothing "spiritual" has happened. The fact that you got through the day is spiritual. Where do you think your energy came from? Let it flow, let it grow, meditate daily, and accept totally that it is happening. Know with a certainty that there is a time for it all to come into its perfect fruition. You are building toward it; and as you let it grow, know that on the days when it seems as if nothing is happening, assimilation of that which you have already acquired is occurring. From that, mo re will come.

Whether it is in business, spiritual growth, friendship, or learning, it all relates to interaction. According to the type of that interaction, be it business, children and parents, lovers, spouse—whatever—it is the inner projection of those involved that creates the interaction. I know of two people who can be together for long periods of time and never say a word to each other, and yet, they are in total communication the whole time. You must be careful that the projection that you put out is realistic. Do not expect too much too soon. Believe in yourself enough to say: What I have to offer is good; what I am is good; I am a good person.

If you really listen to what the other person says, you are helping that person to interact with you. Communication on any level calls for accepting yourself as you are and knowing that that is enough to share. The three-year-old that comes up and tells you of some incident in their life fully accepts that they are an important person with an important message and expects that you are going to give them the time to be heard. Do the same for yourself. Know that what you have is precious, that who you are is precious, and that when you permit that to interact with another on any level, it is a true sharing. In other words, you are not on trial. Unless you are projecting some fantasy, you are going to have the degree of relationship that is right and perfect for that moment. If you are trying to make the communication and exchange more than it really is supposed to be at that point in time, you will not achieve relaxed communication.

When you meet someone you enjoy, don't immediately start wondering if they like you and if you will ever see them again. Recall the incident as a pleasant moment. When that moment is relaxing and enjoyable, you will be more apt to find yourself with the opportunity to be together again.

Remember that your thoughts are powerful things. Start thinking doubtfully, and you will flounder. Instead, remember that you are unique and, therefore, special.

CHAPTER IV

RELATIONSHIPS

Every time you associate with someone, no matter on what level, you are having a relationship. You are learning something about another, something about how they think; and you are learning to share experiences and energies. That all encompasses a relationship.

All relationships are based on certain ingredients, and a good relationship interacts with all levels of the being. Therefore, if you are to have a successful relationship, you must show respect, for respect is the very essence that permits a relationship to exist. By respecting another, their individuality, their uniqueness, you accept them. In that acceptance, you permit a relationship to form. What that relationship will become is based on how you feel in that space.

A relationship is based on mind, body, and spirit. The emotions, of course, are a part of that. A relationship that is purely physical, without any mental or spiritual sharing, is without depth and cannot survive. It will survive only as long as body chemistry exists. Inasmuch as the only absolute in your universe is change, you must respect the idea that you are not going to be the same person throughout a relationship. You are going to encounter differences and changes as each party grows.

When a relationship is expected to be the same from its beginning to its end, it immediately puts you under a strain; for if you are a unique and wonderful being who is growing, you cannot remain the same. If you did, you would all be running around in diapers. You have to permit the growth. When you come together, there is a certain amount of fear and mistrust, because you do not know how vulnerable you will choose to be. How well are you going to let someone know you? How well are you going to permit yourself to know that person? Are your relationships all based on a single experience, or a single interest, or is there more? Are all the good days and the bad days equally respected?

If you have a genuine relationship, do not expect that there will not be bad days. There are going to be days when you are not the same person, and there are going to be days when you are not sure you want that relationship. It does not matter whether it is a relationship between a man and a woman, a relationship with your boss, or a relationship with a friend. There are days when the energies are not in synchronization. That does not mean that the relationship has gone sour. It means that if the respect is there, if there is acceptance of yourself as a unique individual, you will not be afraid to say, "Today wasn't my dream day, but it doesn't change what exists."

When we speak of a love relationship, you must recognize that love is the ring of unity that rests beneath the diversity of the personality. In that unity of love, you withstand the idiosyncrasies of the personality and the ego. Love is not a bartering system. Love is not a check list that says if you do this, I'll do that. Love is not a check list that says you're going to wait to see how much you are given before you will willingly give. Love is a sharing. To have a good relationship is to know yourself; and in knowing yourself, you feel good enough about yourself to share without fearing that somebody will control you. Love is not a domination, it is not a leeching, it is a sharing. You can only share what you are. The first step to a good relationship then is to know who you are, what you are, and where you want to go with it.

A relationship cannot be based on external values. It does not matter whether it is a job, a lover, or a spouse. Your value system must come from within the self. A compatibility of value systems with another must be recognized from within. No person can make you whole; and if you think they can, you are wrong. Your success and your value is based on *you.* If you will recognize the beauty of yourself, that you are a unique individual, that your beauty is the reality of yourself, then your sharing of those qualities is easily done.

Most people roll play. They try to be what somebody thinks they should be. They try to be what the society or the culture says is right. If you try to live by a standard created by another which does not agree with your value system, you will find inner conflict.

A relationship is based on caring; and if it is with a business, there has to be a caring about the business. If you have a job and your only thought is how little you can do for as much as you can get, you are creating a very bad relationship with that job; and it is never going to give you satisfaction. Try thanking the job for whatever it is giving you, try becoming friends with it for a while, try seeing joy in what you give to it, and you will find the atmosphere of the job will begin to change. You will find yourself much more alive and much more fulfilled.

In working situations in your culture and society, the advancement process very often has a certain pattern. That pattern of advancement is not always to the well-being of the individual. Somebody can be an excellent worker in a given area and because the pattern of advancement says the next move is to management, they advance to that position. Their abilities may not lie in management but in production. It would be far better to permit the person to remain in the space they do well in and give them recognition for the value of the job well done. Monetary increase would be indication of a prestige that goes with doing well. That is a pattern that is healthy in business. That is a pattern that is healthy in relationships. Why not let an individual be that which he or she does well?

A lot of patterns in your world are changing. Some men have preferred to become much more domestic, and a lot of women are going out and capturing the business world. Do you know why? It is the balancing of the sexes. It does not take away your masculinity or your femininity, but it takes away the fear for a man to be gentle and for a woman to be strong. It takes away the stereotype that says you must perform in a certain way.

To relate or to be together is to form an acceptance pattern based on what you have. A relationship has to move beyond the white picket fence, the two cars, two dogs, one cat, and three gold fish sort of thing. Your relationship has to be based on what you have and the reality of it. Whenever there is a problem in a relationship, you have to peel back the emotion and look at the facts, because it is only the facts of any situation that can make it move. It does not matter whether you are dealing with the budget, personalities, or whatever, you have to look at what is there and deal with that. You have to permit that growth to occur by acceptance. By accepting that you may not know it all and that they may know it, you create a space of acceptance between you. That movement can make a very great difference. There will be times when you *will* know and, again, acceptance will be the answer. See a relationship as a living, breathing thing. Do not see it as something purchased like a loaf of bread. It is something you work at all the time. The only place that you can change a relationship is in yourself. You cannot mold another unless they choose to be molded.

Many marriage ceremonies today do not promise anything; they merely accept what is already there. They offer to protect, to guide, and to help. Understand that at any point in time, the promises you make and the actions you take, are based on your consciousness level and emotional level of that moment and that time. When one loves, it sounds very logical to promise to love forever—and who says it cannot happen? Fear that the promise might not be real already says that it is not. The promise comes from the depth of the self. It is real. It may, however, in the course of the relationship take new perspectives. Marriage should never be entered into lightly without forethought. Your thoughts will become your reality.

Do not feel disheartened if you experience frustration and disappointment when your expectations do not work out. It is not that something is not right, but that the understanding of the *needs of each other* are not yet fully understood in certain areas. The acceptance of those needs has yet to be fully realized. A marriage is based on trust and love, respect for each other, and the willingness to let each other grow. The changing dimensions of your love over the years enhances it. It does not end it.

In relationships, one of the greatest traps is your thinking that because you are in love, someone is going to know what your needs are. People assume that someone who loves them will automatically know their every need. Not so! The point is that in any relationship, you must let your needs be known. You must say you need to be touched, or you don't like to be touched, or you need space, you need room to breathe. In every relationship, there has to be space in which you can be away from it. You can be right in the same room but not obligated to talk, not obligated to participate, but permitted the space you need to be yourself. This in no way means a lack of love or a weakening of the relationship. It means letting the relationship breathe.

If the relationship becomes so cloying that it begins to

smother, after a while you feel trapped. Many times when something is not working, it is because, at that moment, space is needed but neither has said so. Each part is afraid to say it, but they both want the other to know it. The resentment that builds because the need is not recognized becomes anger. It builds into something that has no relationship to the original thing at all. Let your needs be known right in the beginning.

Very often it is a small thing that drives someone crazy in a relationship. It may be a habit. Maybe it is leaving the cover off the toothpaste. A marriage coming to an end over the toothpaste cap! The toothpaste cap is not what one is really angry about. All the pent up things inside have finally found something to blame it on. When you are discontent in any situation, you must ask yourself why. Ask yourself what *your* attitude in the situation is and not who did what to you. See how *you* are handling it. Are you looking at the facts and dealing with them?

In any relationship, there will be times when things do not seem to go well. It does not mean the relationship is not a good one; it only means that a communication system between you has not been worked out yet. No relationship can be based on a taking. A relationship cannot be based on somebody filling only their own needs. It has to be a sharing. When you hear somebody pulling out the list of everything somebody did or did not do for them, you can be very suspicious that that individual is not a sharing person in the relationship.

The best time to discover these things about a person is

before the marriage. That's what engagements are all about. The right reason for marriage is love. Mind, body, and spirit sharing love together. Many people have married for other reasons, but if love isn't there, it is harder. There are some who marry for security and protection and later learn to love their partner very much. However, if a person marries because someone is a "good catch," they are looking for trouble. They can't stand the individual, but the income is great. How can something like that be expected to work? Don't become enamored of the material aspects. Be sure it is the right person first.

There are several misconceptions about relationships. One is that if you have known someone in another life, you have to be madly in love with them in this life. You were married once before so this is it. Not so! You may come back to have a totally different kind of relationship in this life. Certain emotional memories sometimes surface, called forth by similar instances occurring in the present. For instance, you may have experienced a loving, happy incident in the time of new mown hay. If you smell new mown hay in another life, all the feelings of love come welling up in you. You may be standing all alone, but suddenly the need to love will be there. It is the emotional memory, but not necessarily the conscious understanding of the circumstances, that are carried forth. Very often people will choose to come back together, and they will be together in some capacity. Sometimes it will be the same, sometimes not, but the past influences do very definitely affect how you handle things. They bring you tendencies. How you work with them in this life depends on the energy and the attitude you have toward those tendencies now.

You may have previously determined to work something out together with someone in this lifetime. When you enter the physical world, you are under the jurisdiction of free will in which the conscious mind is permitted to make decisions. You also begin to develop the ego personality aspect of yourself, and that, in turn, encourages decision from the ego aspect of your personality. You are not left without the knowledge of what you came to accomplish, but you have to go inward to find it. It is in the superconscious mind. It is in the soul of you. When you take time to be still, you find it.

Very often one person will decide to handle it and another will not. You cannot revert to the blame system. You cannot say, "Ah hah! I'm doing it, but you're not!" Then you are judging, and that right belongs to the universal law, not to you. Your divine right of discernment says it is not working. You have tried, therefore, you are free of the karma. The law will take care of the judgment. The Law of Cause and Effect is always in motion and cannot be stopped. You will find out the answers if you go inward. You may have experienced meeting someone and being attracted to them. All the while, in your head, an alarm is going off saying no, no, no, and yet you are saying yes, yes, yes. It is because you want *that* at *that* moment. If you truly listen, you are going to back off and pay attention to the fact that it can have some pitfalls. The pitfalls may come from you as much as from them.

Recognize that in life, your relationships build one upon the other. The relationship you had at home within your parent's marriage builds preconceived ideas about marriage.

Without realization, you begin to expect similar behavior in other relationships. If you have known someone who was chronically late in one relationship, you may find yourself ready to jump on anyone who is late in a new relationship.

Very often one person will decide to handle it and another will not. You cannot revert to the blame system. You cannot say, "Ah hah! I'm doing it, but you're not!" Then you are judging, and that right belongs to the universal law, not to you. Your divine right of discernment says it is not working. You have tried, therefore, you are free of the karma. The law will take care of the judgment. The Law of Cause and Effect is always in motion and cannot be stopped. You will find out the answers if you go inward. You may have experienced meeting someone and being attracted to them. All the while, in your head, an alarm is going off saying no, no, no, and yet you are saying yes, yes, yes. It is because you want *that* at *that* moment. If you truly listen, you are going to back off and pay attention to the fact that it can have some pitfalls. The pitfalls may come from you as much as from them.

Recognize that in life, your relationships build one upon the other. The relationship you had at home within your parent's marriage builds preconceived ideas about marriage. Without realization, you begin to expect similar behavior in other relationships. If you have known someone who was chronically late in one relationship, you may find yourself ready to jump on anyone who is late in a new relationship. The attitude being, "I knew it; it's just like before!"

If you have ended a relationship, whether a love affair, a

marriage—whatever—you must permit yourself time to know yourself. You are not the same person any longer by the very experience of that relationship. You must come to grips with your needs, who you are, and what you share or do not share. Then you move with that new understanding toward a new relationship. Don't rush into relationships. Be willing to have friends and enjoy them. When that is ready to deepen, you will know it.

When two people with families from a previous relationship come together and form a new unit, several things happen. First you have chaos. The two families are groups of individuals and within those groups of individuals, there are exchanges of energy. When those packages come together to share, there is going to be adjustments. Sometimes they are going to feel that one is not getting enough attention, or the other one is getting too much attention. If you will have open council periodically with productive non-defensive communication, it will help. Children must be permitted to express what they feel so that they are not building explosive energies inside. You will then find the means to harmony. Knowing they will be listened to helps children begin to trust intercommunication.

Take time in a group of that sort to individually have time with each one. It can be as simple as going to one and saying you're glad they are in your life. Periodically ask them to help you make a decision so they know they are a valid participant in a family unit. The biggest mistake that can possibly be made is to try to buy harmony by pampering and catering to every whim, because that is forming false values. Instead, say, "Tough luck! This month it can't

be. These are the alternatives, which one do you want?"
want?" Above all, do not personalize everything that is
said, because in frustrating moments, things are going to be
spit out that they do not really mean. It is their hurt of the
moment talking. When it happens, you just say you'll talk
about it later and then give them a hug.

Some of the strongest relationships in the world are
built from friendships. Why? Because in the friendship, the
idiosyncrasies of the personalities are worked out, and the
love is free to bloom. Did you ever notice that two people
can be the best of friends and suddenly they find they are in
love and become frightened? Instead of waking up and
being joyous, they are looking the situation over to be sure
it is not a big trap. Why? Because of the vulnerability. The
relationship of friendship is an exchange in which you do
not feel as confined. A one-on-one relationship—that you
call love—makes you vulnerable. Now you can be hurt,
now you're not as much in control. The moment that there
is intimacy, a sexual exchange, you are really vulnerable.
What you have done is relinquish yourself to another. It
does not matter whether you are the male or the female,
there is a sense of no longer being in control. It does not
make any difference. You have given of yourself, and now
it is spooky. Now you are concerned about what happens
next. The pressure is on. A relationship truly needs some
time to determine whether it is going to really be one that
can be a comfortable and joyous experience.

Suppose you suddenly meet someone and wonder if this
one might be the one. If you are an open, warm person, you
do not see every person as "it." You do not try to make just

anyone that person, but you give the people you meet a chance to open themselves to you and you to them. If you understand that you often approach a relationship with pre-conceived ideas, you will realize what a blockage that can be. You can only see a relationship from your own precon-ceived perspective. You can only see *your* idea of a rela-tionship. If your idea of relationships has proven unfulfill-ing, you will anticipate the same again. You must give the relationship time to grow so you can see the differences. It is very important for you to be willing to accept the fact that you can have a good relationship. Most people treat relationships as, "If I don't have one, I'm a failure." Did you ever think that there are some relationships you are bet-ter off without? Do not be afraid when a relationship seems to fade or ends.

When somebody says, "Nobody loves me," the first questions I have to ask is, "Are you loveable?" Who can love someone who is not loveable? If you are not loveable, why do you want to be that way? Look at what *you* have done to *you*. You were born loveable. Let it grow, let it become larger in you.

Body chemistry can get you in trouble, because you do not want to wait to see if you can really talk to the person. Look beyond the body chemistry. Make sure there is some-thing else. Then you will have something that lasts. If it is based only on body chemistry, it can only last as long as the body chemistry remains.

When that right person comes along, it will be based on more than one level. There will be a feeling of friendship, of caring, and of interest. If you meet someone and they are not the least bit interested in you, or what you are interested in, you have to ask yourself if that is enough. Also be sure that you *really are* interested in them and their interests. Don't pretend interest when it really isn't there. This is important because it is a sharing. The person who pretends to love classical music when they really don't is trying to have a relationship based on deceit.

If a person is only sexually interested in you, it is not enough, because sex is not love. Sex is *one* expression of love, but there are many other expressions. When you meet someone and you think of them as a potential friend, as the friendship develops, let the relationship grow to where you can feel at ease with each other. Let a sense of acceptance grow with each other. From there, you will begin to have deeper feelings and come to better know what is right for you. You can be interested in different things, but the sharing of those things is what counts. You can learn new interests, but they must be real not false.

There are some people who meet each other and instantly know this is it because they are souls who have been looking for each other. Even though everyone thinks that they have that in them, not everyone does. It is a very special thing when two souls seek each other. When that happens, there is no doubt in the world on any level, and the problems that exist between them can always be worked out because of the strong focus that is there. The soul level is there, the mental level is there, and the body level is there. You may meet someone and be attracted to them, and that is wonderful—so be friends. Find out more about that individual so that you know whether there is a sharing that can become more.

When you meet somebody, whether you realize it or not, you are projecting a preconceived image on them. You are projecting something you want them to be. Very early in a relationship, you can still convince yourself that that is what they really are. Later on, you take another look and say they are failing you, that they are not what you saw in them. It is your preconceived image that has failed. Both parties do this. The reason a relationship needs time is so that both parties can find out whether they are dealing with fantasies or with reality. If people are aware that everyone changes and that the growth pattern along the way does not have to be disastrous, it can be a growth that is very much a growing closer as opposed to growing apart. The more people understand what they want when they go into a relationship, the stronger the relationship is. When both parties express their needs to each other, they can better see if they are capable of answering them.

Semantics are important in relationships. A word means one thing to one person and something else to another. What is a relationship? To one person that word may mean deep commitment and to somebody else it may mean a casual interlude. You had better know that you are using the same words in the same context. It is important to know that what you are saying and what you are feeling is being understood in the same way that you are saying or feeling it. The only way they are going to know that is if you express it.

People go through a whole lifetime wanting something

badly in a relationship, yet being so stubborn that they will never say they want it. It does not necessarily mean a material thing. Maybe it means flowers, maybe it means breakfast in bed, maybe it means buttons on shirts, but it is an expectation they have inside in relationship to love. "Love means this, and I've waited all my life for this fool to do it, and he or she hasn't." Well, of course not! You have never let them know. Having wine at a celebration can create the assumption that it goes with every celebration. Sometimes you have to say you prefer coffee. You have to let it be known. You have to communicate not only your needs or desires, but also other things. Try communicating how proud you are of each other's accomplishments.

What happens when one likes the ballet and one likes to bowl? Maybe you go bowling one month and to the ballet the next. Maybe you say, "Hey, you go and enjoy what you like with your friends, and I'll enjoy with mine what I like." If you take that approach, do not see it as a lack of love, do not see it as a desertion. See it as the space that is needed to know that you still exist as individuals. You have not been lost in the shuffle somewhere. In a relationship, you can begin to feel as if you have been lost in the shuffle somewhere. When you do things separately, *share the experi -ence.*

The important thing to remember is that love functions on all levels. Love is the energy that you were created in, for, with, and to. It is the strongest energy in the universe. It is the energy that can overcome all things. It exists and permeates all things. Seek to enjoy the sharing of you and let whatever is to grow from that relationship grow.

In a relationship where one person is more giving, accepting, and loving than the other, you have to ask why. If they are trying to buy it by being giving, loving, and accepting, they are not really giving, loving, and accepting, they are playing a role. They are becoming the martyr of the future. Some people give because they love to give. They are totally comfortable in giving, and they expect nothing in return. Anyone who gives with a string attached to it is not giving, they are anticipating. There is a big difference. You have to ask yourself what you think of as loving and giving.

You have little birds called pigeons. They do their ritual dances and their snuggling and cooing when they are together. It is not very different from people. Does not everyone who thinks they want to attract someone do a ritual dance? Do they not snuggle a little bit? There is always a sharing. There is always the announcement, "I'm ready, I need you." There is always the announcement that something is felt, and there is always the reaching out to touch. No matter what world it is, no matter what universe, no matter what the shape or form, one goes through the rituals.

You have to learn the code of the individual. Some people bring flowers as an expression of love, and some people change the oil in the car, but they are both acts of love. Sometimes you have to know that you are being told you are loved, though not in the mode you expected. Then you have to say, "Wait a minute. I love the fresh oil in the car. It makes me feel safe. I also love to receive flowers."

Look at yourself and ask if you are being honest with

yourself. Honesty is knowing what you are really putting into the relationship and what you are really expecting out of it. It is not roll playing. Have you ever seen people who become the greatest skier in the world because the one they are in love with at the moment loves to ski; and if the next one that comes along is a gourmet cook, they become the greatest cook in the world? By the time they are done, they are going to be the best at everything, but they are not going to know who they are until they find out what *they* want to do.

What if you feel lack of respect in a relationship? The first place to find out what is wrong is in yourself. Why do you feel you are not respected? If you do not feel respected, you *could* be interpreting respect as agreeing with you all the time. If, on the other hand, that disrespect is blatant, if you don't count, or are being put down constantly, *ask yourself why you tolerate it.*

In many family units, the parents and children make an agreement to come together while on the other side. Once you are on this side you say, "Why in the name of heaven would I choose these parents?" Or, "Why in the name of heaven would I choose these children?" That is looking at the personality aspect. Remember that the decisions made before you came into the world are based on soul. They are based on what you need to learn and grow by, so the *great - est antagonist* in your life can sometimes be your *greatest teacher.*

In a relationship between a parent and a child, if each respects the space of the other, it will be a friendship. The greatest honor a parent can have is eventually not being though of as a parent but as a friend. When you become your children's friend, you are releasing them. You have stopped using the check-list. You have to let them become independent, *but you must also let you be independent.* You cannot get lost in the shuffle.

There is a wonderful word in your world. It is called "no." Saying no in any kind of a relationship at the right time can cause tremendous peace. "No, it is not convenient for me to drive some place right now." "No, I don't like that kind of book." Does that make you less of a person? Does it make you less lovable? If being loved is based on never saying no, it is not love in the first place. You have not lost a blessed thing; for if there is love, there is respect for the unique individual in that love.

Two people have come together in love, marry, and have children. Their whole life goes into the children. When the children are grown and leave, the parents look at each other and say, "Who are you?" because they have lost touch with each other. They are two strangers. A relationship in a family sense has to have equal time for the parents as well as for the child. The parents have to have "we" time. Many people like to become a martyr to their children. "I worked my fingers to the bone for you." No, you did it because you thought it made you a good person. Do not con yourselves. You do things in life because you see it in relationship to you and your image. Love your children, but do not see them alone as your life. It is unfair to you, and it is unfair to them.

In life, you very often will try to assist others. Try to help them, but don't take on what is rightfully theirs. Know that you cannot live another's life for them. You can make a suggestion based on your own experience, but they must make their decisions and must go through whatever they have to go through. Every decision has a responsibility and an action that follows it. Therefore, they must take the responsibility for those decisions.

To say, "Listen, I went through this, and I ended up burned, so be careful," can be helpful. Do not get upset if your advice is not followed. You can advise, you can assist, you can guide, but you cannot live another person's life.

Soul mates are over rated. People sit around and wait for this person to show up to make their life whole. They are already placing such expectation on that person that when they find them, they are perplexed. Their preconceived idea was the knight in shining armor, or the wonderful maiden with the long hair, who would answer all their needs. Realize that the only one who can make it right for you is *you*. Everyone is here as a brother to the other at soul level. *You*, however, are responsible for *your* growth. Also, a soul mate is not necessarily a male/female relationship, or a love relationship. It can be your boss, it can be anybody. They are there to assist in some form.

Do not go around saying, "I want to attract a soul mate." Say, "I want a right and perfect relationship in my life," and that is what you will find. Know that it is coming to you.

110

Any relationship you were in was not *all* bad, or you would not have been in it in the first place. There is something that you have gained from it. You have gained some growth or understanding along the way. Do not pretend that the relationship did not exist. If you do, you are saying *you did not exist* for that period of time. Instead, look at your part in the relationship honestly: learn from it, bless it, thank it for its lesson, and let it go. Now you can focus your energy on the new and wonderful things yet to come.

Brotherhood cannot be built on being a "yes man." It cannot be built on always accepting other people's values, but it can be created by the realization that other people's values can merge with yours and be creatively progressive. They do not have to be adverse.

It is important to recognize and remember that for a relationship to be a lasting one, it has to function on more than one level. In a job situation, you may feel comfortable with a job in the beginning but eventually begin to feel bored because the mind is not stimulated enough. It becomes a rut that causes you to look for new stimuli. Unfortunately, man has the tendency to think that the search for new stimuli is not enough. He has to have a rationale for making change, so he immediately looks for all the negatives in the job he once enjoyed. If you are looking for them, they are there, of course. He then begins to create friction with his fellow employees and with his boss. He tends to make the job a miserable place, so now he has an absolutely clear rationale for leaving. He puts himself and everyone else through a great deal of trouble in order to

111

make it miserable enough for it to be all right to leave. In reality, he has the absolute right to leave. These are not deliberate conscious acts, but they are a trap that people fall into subconsciously.

In the relationship of parent and child, this very same thing occurs. A maturing child may begin to need more space. Rather than declare this openly, they begin to seek everything negative about the home in order to have valid reasons for leaving.

We all do the same thing in varying forms. We try to manifest a rationale for that which we want to do. Spouses very often do the same thing. When a relationship is in trouble, instead of recognizing that it must have a bases within that could be looked at and understood, they begin to blame the relationship for all that is wrong. They do not have a rationale for why they feel the way they do, so one must be created which relieves them of full responsibility.

You are a unique energy. You are unique in your own right and have the right to your own fulfillment. Unfortunately, in relationships, no matter what kind they are, there is a tendency to constantly look to see if you are being fulfilled. "What's in it for me?" Remember the other parties in the relationship are unique as well. Fulfillment must be for each participant, not for one alone.

What is fulfillment? Fulfillment changes, even as you change. A child is very content with a toy. An adult will not be. Children play with baby dolls, adults want grownup ones. Children play with small cars, adults want big ones; but in a sense, they are also toys. They are things to make them happy. The only difference is that, hopefully, the adult sees that there is a responsibility that goes with it a little bit more clearly than a child.

As fulfillment changes day to day, it might seem to be nebulous. Fulfillment is not always the same. There are degrees of fulfillment. If you have a feeling of accomplishment, or if you have a feeling of contentment and peace, you have had a day of fulfillment. Many people think fulfillment is something that permits them to "have." Fulfillment, however, comes from inside the self. It is how you use your energy, how you prove to yourself your ability to accomplish. Feel fulfillment at each step on the way to a goal. Don't see just the final outcome as the only place you can be fulfilled.

Try to recognize accomplishment on all levels in your life each day. One person might say, "I managed to tolerate someone that most people could not possibly stand." In essence, that is an accomplishment. "I managed to hold my temper when I did not want to." Maybe it is something as simple as, "I saw the sunrise." Progressive action does not mean great accomplishment necessarily. It means a sense of having used your potential and your ability in some way.

Understand that when you are interacting with another person, you very often role-play. The role-playing very often stems from wanting to be like that person. Gradually you begin to become someone else. If a relationship is being formed on your being someone else, eventually you are going to discover that you are not in a relationship at all. When you finally tire of trying to be their energy, you will find yourselves strangers with no understanding of each other at all. You have not had a true relationship at all.

The tendency—especially in a new relationship—is to role-play. Somewhere along the line, you have to be honest with each other because, to succeed, a relationship has to be based on honesty and respect. Somewhere along the line you may have to say, "I dislike pre-Columbian art," or, "I don't really like to run." Somewhere along the line you have to be yourself.

From the time you are a child, you are programmed from outside yourself by external influences. You accept them as your reality, and then one day discover that there are parts of you you have yet to discover and use. Very often someone comes along and pushes a button in you; and all of a sudden, there is another realization revealed. There is a new feeling about yourself, a new understanding, a new excitement. Accept that other part of you as a gift and use it to know yourself better.

If a relationship is a real one, there is an *encouragement* of the potential of the other rather than a *competitiveness* with the potential of another. The realization and acceptance that someone else can also be talented and achieve without it diminishing your own abilities is a great growth. It can be the recognition that you can be as proud of somebody else's accomplishment as you can of your own.

When there is trouble in a relationship, there is a tendency to immediately list in your mind the negatives of the other individual. You go around waiting and watching for them to make an error so that you can jump on them and say, "Aha! You see? You did it again." If you spent the same amount of time counting the good in that person, you would soon find out that things weren't as bad as you thought. There are times when you have to hold back the ego and emotions long enough to look at the facts.

Think of a can of sardines. When you put that key in the can and roll back the lid, there they are all in a row. You can see that they are stacked one on top of the other. You cannot deny them; they are jammed in there as tight as can be. The next time you are in a difficult situation, think of those sardines. You are that can and the lid is the emotions that keep the real contents hidden. Place your power—your key—in that lid and roll back your emotions and reveal the facts of the situation. There are things relating to the situation that you have piled one on top of the other until you are jammed full of emotional reactions. Facts are the only things you can work with, and the facts are neither right nor wrong. They simply state the reality of the situation. Instead of having yourself totally hidden in the emotion, peel back your lid and recognize the facts. Deal with those, and your troubles begin to fade.

When a relationship has become painful, and you have honestly looked at your participation in it, you will have realized what the facts are. Examine not what you want or do not want, not what you thought was fair or unfair, but

115

what the facts say. No relationship is meant to remain when it causes nothing but pain for those involved in it. A relationship that is destroying your own unique individuality and destroying the other person's as well serves no benefit. The point you must remember is that the ego gets in the way. The ego would rather suffer than admit an ending. You have to be willing to step back from the emotional part and look at the facts.

There is a magic ingredient in a relationship. The magic ingredient is the thing that permitted each of you to respond to the other. When it is there for both parties, the relationship is marvelous. If it is not there for one party, you cannot make them have it. You are constantly changing, growing, and moving in your progression in life. Two people who come together euphorically at one point may, for some reason, discover later that the magic has gone out of one of them. The other will feel the pain more because they are still trying to fan the ember; but at some given point, they have to recognize that the ember is not going to come back to a flame, and they must be willing to let it go. Realize that when we say you recognize that the magic is gone, it means you have *tried your best* to solve the problems but have not succeeded in rekindling the magic. It is then that you are free to let it go.

The relationship that is let go in hatred creates a karmic pattern for *the individual who is hating and vengeful*. There are times when you have to realize that it is not possible to sail in the present if you are still anchored in the past. You have to slip anchor and let yourself sail again. There is no such thing as there being only one person in the world for someone. Your world is an exchange of energies, and there are many, many people in the world who can give you happiness.

There are many you can give happiness to. The thing you have to be very careful about is that you not become so enamored of misery that you go around using it as an excuse for not moving ahead with life. "There will never be another person in my life." When you say that, you are really using that person as an escape route. You do not want to go through that which you have to go through to have another relationship, which means facing yourself. That is the one that nobody wants to face. Notice how you can tell everybody else what to do; but when it comes to yourself, it is a whole different story. You are a very nice person, and you are very nice to know. *You* should not be afraid to look *you* square in the eye. My suggestion is: Turn and face the tiger; and if the tiger is *you*, face that too. There is no relationship—good, bad, or indifferent—in your life that does not teach you something. There is no relationship that does not let you grow. In that growth, you are able to look back and know the things that you do not want to repeat in your life. They were things both good and bad, but they still showed you something.

Semantics are interesting. Have you ever looked at words over the years and seen how the meaning of a word has changed? Especially in what you call "slang." You say something is "cool" and something is "hot." At different times it means different things. If a person has a particular desire for you, if their need from you is strong, they will interpret what you are saying the way they *want* to hear it. They hear *your* words through *their* needs.

I hear people say, "My love is strong enough for both of us." It does not work that way because, eventually, being a human being, you need something back. There has to be some way that you are feeling loved. If you are not, you are going to begin to feel resentment, and you are going to begin to get angry. You have an expression in your world, "Don't beat a dead horse." It is not going to get up and run. A dead relationship is not going to get up and run either. The only place you can love enough for both of you is with young children, because you understand their lack of comprehension.

A relationship that permits the growth of the individuals within it will be a forever relationship. The new Age does not mean that forever relationships are not supposed to be, but it means that you will better recognize the growth and the movement in that relationship. You will not expect it to be as it was when you first came together. Heaven forbid you should go through your whole life the way it was when you first came together. You would look back and feel absolutely stagnated.

A relationship is meant to grow. It is meant to change its face and get better and better with each face change. It is meant to be a flexible, giving, and sharing thing. When someone refuses to see through anyone's eyes but their own, they are limiting the relationship; and it cannot

118

become something that is lasting. It cannot be a one way street.

One of the saddest things in your world is that people get a fixed idea of what a perfect relationship is. These usually relate to outer appearances. They have to be 5'2", or 6'5", or blue-eyed, or red-haired, etc., etc., etc. If you would ask for a right and perfect person for you and then be truly in touch with that which comes to you, you would also see the inner qualities. You would not be shutting out of your life someone who is very right for you because the hair color isn't right.

There are many reasons why some people may *choose* to stay together even if they feel something is missing. Some people can successfully say, "There's nothing here that I call magic, but we're accustomed to each other enough that we can co-exist together without animosity." If animosity exists, they are only destroying themselves. Have you heard the phrase, "We stayed together for the children."? That statement makes me want to wince. Don't do it unless you can be cordial to each other. Children are totally aware of the energies of anger in the household, and an unexplained anger in a household makes them assume they are responsible for it. That is the only way they see things, and it gets very uneasy for them. That does not mean that you are supposed to take the children aside and describe your mate to them in horrible terms. If you separate, explain to them that sometimes adults outgrow each other and find themselves incompatible. Let them know it has nothing to do with your love for them. Do not ask children to take sides. That is a horrible thing to do to them.

Separation has to be a free-will choice, because God granted free will and He will not rescind it. What matters is what you are going to do to each other during that time. If the relationship is one-upsmanship and destructive all the way, it is not a relationship. In that case, you might as well be out of it.

There is no relationship in the whole world where the parties involved do not dislike each other some time along the way. The realization that there is more than today's misery, anger, or sense of failure sees them through. Only the two people in it can determine whether they can alter the situation to make it harmonious.

One thing that you have to recognize is that there is a difference between *disliking by the divine right of discern - ment* and *prejudice*. Each is a totally different thing. If your dislike of someone is based on your own sense of what everyone else *should* do, whether it is right for them or not, that is a judgement. If that disliking is because in some way it feels destructive to you on the soul level, that is discernment; and there is a difference.

Sometimes there is a feeling between two people that makes them light up and lets them see each other as beautiful. This is magic. Somewhere deep inside you, you sense the knight in shining armor or the maiden in the tower with the long, long hair. It is something that happens inside. It is a union between those two energies that occurs, and it does not happen just on a sexual basis. It goes deeper than that. There is a caring beyond the body chemistry. That is why it is magic, because it deeply involves *the whole being*. We use the word magic because magic lets something happen. The magic is that which transpires between the two people and transforms them.

Whenever that feeling is present, the individuals will always accomplish more. They will take better care of themselves; they will be happier in life. They will probably try to do more with their lives than they ever did before because somebody believes in them. It is a very beautiful thing to behold. It does exist in the world, it really does.

Interaction in the world is always a growth pattern. If you learn by yourself, you are interacting with you. You cannot go through life without relating. It does not have to be a personal one-to-one relationship; you are going to interact with the bus driver, the dentist, your friends, and even your so-called enemies. No matter what, you are going to have relationships in your life because interaction of energy and energy exchange is a growth factor. What quality of relationship they are is up to you.

It is very important for children to respect themselves and to make decisions, because that is something they are going to have to do for the rest of their lives. One way children develop respect is by your listening to them. Many parents do not listen to their children. The child talks and the parent's mind is in ten other places. The amount of time spent with a child should be what you call "quality" time.

Make it a time in which you *really* hear what the child is saying. Put yourself on their level for a few minutes and listen. Do not talk *down* to them, but talk *with* them at their level. As you do this, you will develop a trust with that child and a respect that will be with you long after that child becomes an adult.

A great deal of a child's training comes from outside the home, but there are certain qualities of a moral nature, qualities of love and sharing, that can *only* be developed in the home. They cannot be developed anywhere else. Respect for their bodies has to be developed in the home. Clinical teaching in classes is one thing, but understanding that their bodies are something very special is quite another. They have to learn a full sense of respect for their mind, body, and spirit. In the future, the home will take back many of the responsibilities that have been put elsewhere. Home should be a nurturing place that is not external but internal. That can only happen when you are in close contact with your children.

Do not let children grow up not knowing how to make a decision. Children should not grow up being told what to do every minute of their lives. They must learn how to make decisions. You cannot throw them out into the world at a given age and say, "Now go be an adult." If they have never had any training in being an adult, how are they going to be one?

Children learn by watching the parents. How can a child be expected to be courteous if parents do not treat each other in a courteous manner? A positive parental model and a nurturing atmosphere that a family unit creates is the most important ingredient you can give your children to be able to survive in the world.

No matter how loving that home is, children are going to want to leave it to explore away from it. That is normal. The birds kick their young out as soon as they can fly. They have the right idea. Parents try to hold onto the children, and the reason they do that is because, very often, they have started to live *through* the children. They have not seen their children as individuals or as separate entities, but as an extension of themselves. The parents put so much time and energy into the children that they forget that they are people.

Let your children know and understand that parents are unique and wonderful individuals who love them. They are individuals who have a right to some of the same things the child has. The child has time to play with friends, and mother and father also have the right to play with friends. You teach them to respect each other's needs. In that manner, the child and the parent both grow up respecting each other's space. All parents do a lot of growing up with their children. Having learned from each other, both will understand the other better.

Treat children as adults with regard to respect and honesty. You let them understand it in the manner their age can comprehend. They can touch whatever you are touching at some level, but it is the openness, the honesty, and the respect that is so important.

When children are ill or overcoming a great difficulty, they have the right to dignity, a right to feel they are a person who can still function. Help them through the situation by not showing *over concern*. Be compassionate but firm. Remember, thoughts are things. They have a power. Let your thoughts be positive and progressive. Help the children understand that they are not a lesser being because they are indisposed.

A child who is handicapped needs to have encouragement toward their ability and potential, not have emphasis put on the handicap. If a child cannot do something in one way, show them another way. Then that child can do more and more. The more children do for themselves, the more confident they become. The more they understand that they are not *someone different*, but are simply someone with a *different way* of doing things, the easier it is for them to work around the handicap and develop a positive attitude. In the desire to help, sometimes too much help is given; and the child never discovers all the other wonderful abilities he or she has.

Facts are the manifested form of truth for a given situation. For instance, if you have four slices of bread, that is how many slices of bread you have. You may need eight slices, but the fact remains that what you *have* is four. The only thing you can do is either figure out how to get more bread or make something with the four slices you have. You can make believe, you can fantasize, you can philosophize, you can do anything you want; there are still certain facts relating to the situation. When you start to rationalize, you get into why you only have four slices of bread, and you start to make excuses for only having four. You begin to try to make the four slices of bread have a reason for being only four slices of bread. They have a reason—you ate the rest. (Maybe the mice ate them?) Just look at the facts and forget the reasons. The reasons are behind you, and you want to move ahead.

In any group situation, two things occur: First, what is the goal of the group? You have to know what the group is for, where it is headed, and why it wants to go there. Secondly, you have to know what your own individual growth is in that group. A group is more than a collection of people coming together to answer only their own needs. The group itself is going to have a goal. Those things have to be understood. Why are you there? In joining a group, are you there for growth, or are you looking for social satisfaction? Go into a group knowing what you need from it and what you expect of it. Ask what the group represents and then respect your own space as well as the collective space of the group as you participate. Sometimes you outgrow a group, and it no longer has what you are looking for. The group itself grows in one direction, and you find your interest growing in another. That does not mean there is anything wrong with either the group or you.

There are varying approaches to growth in a group. There are some people who prefer a mental approach; there are some people who prefer a discussion; there are some people who prefer a meditation. There are varying ways to approach growth patterns, but you have to know what is right for you. There is nothing wrong with changing your association with a group. If that group is no longer answering your growth pattern, move to a new group. It is also important for people in a group situation, knowing the goal of the group, to be willing to move with the group goal. If you know that a group is coming together to study a certain material, then you must determine whether you are interested in that material. If you do not determine this, you may later find yourself blaming the group because you do not feel fulfilled. In every situation, there is a group goal within which individual goals find growth. Everyone has dual responsibilities both to their own individual growth and the group growth. This gives you the opportunity to grow, not only in your inner space but in interaction space as well.

Throughout his lifetime, man will interact and relate with many things, be that a personal relationship or a business relationship, with children or animals, with friends or so-called foes, the rule is the same—to share who you are with whoever they are. When dealing with the greatest relationship of all—your Universe—the same applies. When you take from the Universe, be willing to give to it. If you are cutting wood, plant some trees.

Here are some keys to a successful relationship:

1. Know who you are. Know your *strong* points and your *weak* points and accept them.

2. Share who you are without preconceived ideas about the other person.

3. Remember that a relationship calls for *listening* as well as talking.

4. Respect each other's space. It is essential in order to not feel threatened.

5. Give it time to grow and include laughter as a means of not getting too up tight. Laugh at yourselves and with each other.

6. Respect people as they are not as you expect they should be.

7. Know with a certainty that you are capable of having excellent relationships, both personal and in business. Accept this as *your* truth.

To act wisely, you must listen wisely.

CHAPTER V

THE NORMALCY OF REJECTION

If I were to ask you what rejection means, there are many responses you could give. It could be the opposite of acceptance, or even feeling unwanted. However, rejection is not something put *on* you, but something *you* accept *for* you. Logic says not everyone is going to like you. Logic says some of your energies will repel and some will attract others. Human nature says, "I want to be liked." When the two are in conflict, the personality self takes over and sees the normal repelling of energy as an affront or an attack, and a feeling of a rejection results. Literally, the only one who can reject you is *you*.

There is an aspect of human nature which feels the need to belong. It has been in effect since the beginning of time. Even herds of animals want to be together. There is safety in numbers. When people come together to share ideas, there is usually a sense of acceptance and belonging because of similar feelings and attitudes. One very often does in a group that which they would not feel secure enough to do alone.

If I want to be obnoxious, I am certainly not going to do it alone and take all the blame. If, however, I can get a group who wants to be obnoxious with me, then we can spread the blame and I can always say, "They did it." It is normal for you as a human to want acceptance. Sometimes to have acceptance you will reject another. How many exclusive clubs are there in the world? How many racial preferences are there in the world? My little group has acceptance, so you keep out. You begin to think that the only way to have acceptance is through creating a subtle form of rejection.

The need to feel exclusively accepted sometimes leads people to feel they truly belong only when someone else is excluded. The need to reject is just as powerful in you as the fear of rejection. The only way that you can take away the need to reject or take away the fear of rejection is to stop fearing. The only way to do that is to believe in you.

If you were to paint everything in a room the same color— floors, ceiling, walls, doors, chairs, people—it would be pretty dull. It might be striking for a moment as shock value; but after that, it would become an irritant because there would be nothing to stimulate movement. There would be nothing to stimulate a sense of something happening. That is why each person has a unique individual energy. In your interactions, in the repelling and the acceptance, you weave a tapestry that is constantly changing.

Have you had a best buddy over the years? Do you have the same best buddy now that you had ten years ago? Some will and some will not because whoever were best buddies at that moment were filling a need in each other. As the growth patterns changed, you moved out of that need for each other and into a need for something else. It does not mean that they are not just as fine a person; it does not reduce the value of either buddy; it merely recognizes that growth brings change. It should not be considered a rejection. At this point in time, the only absolute is change; and if you try to stay in a stagnant place, you will have irritations. You have to accept that there will be changes in your interactions with people. There will be changes in how *you* interact. This does not mean that every one of you will leave the person you are with; it does not mean that at all; but it means you will interact with that person in a different manner. You will not be able to interact with anyone in the same manner that you did in the past. You will either grow *with* the relationship or *away* from it.

It is a very exciting time right now in your world. All the things you ever wanted to do can now be done—unless you reject the thought that it can. There are as many reasons for feeling rejected as there are many reasons for feeling the need to reject another. The strongest rejection powers in your world are handed down from generation to generation. The prejudices, angers, and hatred of the parents are instilled in the child. The child is then ready to reject in turn.

A need to reject or to be rejected can be very strong in

some people. Very often people who not feel good about themselves will seek a reason for feeling that way. They tend to seek a slight in something somebody says. When they do not get the job they wanted, they think they are being picked on because they are not liked. They are not going to look at the logic of it at all, like the man who has made shoes all his life and is now trying to be the president of a computer company. He had better learn about computers first.

People use rejection as an excuse for not facing the issues of themselves and for not facing the changes that need to occur in them. You have to be able to say, "Tomorrow it may be different, but it does not mean that today did not count." Have you ever felt rejected by the rain? Another wet, lousy day—grumble, grumble, grumble. Mother Earth is out to get me. It may not be the most pleasant thing at the moment, but it certainly is helping your reservoirs and crops. It certainly means that you will not have a lack of water at a later point.

Sometimes a rejection occurs to keep you from being embroiled in something you are not suppose to be in, something that you cannot see for the moment. You cannot understand the rejection because you already have a preconceived idea of what is exactly right for you. You are not looking beyond the moment. Every time you feel rejected, if you really look at the reality, you will see that though the situation exists, you may be assuming more than is really there. You are assuming that a rejection is there. If you do not feel good about yourself and somebody tells you your missing a button, your thought may be, "I don't look nice." Do you really want to go around with a button off? In reality, it is not a rejection, but a sign of somebody caring enough to tell you. According to the mood you are in, you will interpret it one way or the other. There is a normalcy in the immediate feeling of rejection, but at that point, you must take it into a new space and permit yourself to look at it in a different way. Permit yourself to see everything that is surrounding the situation.

Suppose you have been a person who has felt rejected all your life, perhaps because your parents felt rejected all their lives. Now your child comes home and says someone yelled at them. What are you going to do? Is your reaction, "No one is going to hurt my child; I'm going right up there and get them." The fact that the child let all the air out of the bus tires has nothing to do with it. *Find out the facts before you accept a feeling of rejection.* The facts may not indicate a rejection at all but the simple reality of the situation in relationship to everyone concerned and in relationship to you as well.

Energies are like magnets; some attract and some repel. It has nothing to do with good or bad; it simply deals with energy types. There will be times in life when you feel uneasy with someone for no apparent reason. You need only to recognize that your energies are not clicking. Don't make more of it than that, and don't feel obligated to tell everyone how uneasy this person makes you feel. That will only make you appear judgmental and small. Tearing someone else down does little to build you up.

Anything that has happened to you is registered in every one of your senses. If you have had an especially pleasant moment in a relationship, it is registered in the sense of touch, smell, sight, taste, and hearing. If an incident occurs where the same energies come up in you again, you will relive those sensory emotions. suppose you have had an experience that was not a particularly happy one? That too has registered. If a friend says he is going to the theater and you ask to go and he responds, "I only have four tickets, I do not have an extra one," you should not feel rejected. The fact that you cannot go does not have anything to do with whether he likes you or not—there are only four tickets. If you let that four tickets situation trigger those old senses, you are going to feel just as rejected as if he had said, "I have fifteen tickets, but I don't want you to go." You have to ask yourself why you are feeling rejected. What is it that is really causing the pain? Is the pain coming from a valid space? Are you refusing to see the reality of the situation?

When someone is unable (for whatever reason) to participate in something with another person or a group of people, part of them accepts that and another part of them feels that somehow they should be able to. There is a feeling that somehow they are being left out.

How do you alter some of the things in you? There is a wonderful number called seven. It is the magic number. It is man and matter united creating a power point that is invisible. If you affirm a new thought in a series of seven, the subconscious reacts. Repeat the new affirmation seven times a day for seven days, seven times and hour for seven hours, or whatever system is convenient for you to work with. The subconscious changes its program by repetition. Whatever you say, the subconscious accepts as fact. It therefore reprograms when it hears the repetitious statement. Statements such as, nothing ever works, everything is wrong, etc., are being programmed in you, by you, as your future. Be careful what you say! Because the subconscious rules the body through the pituitary gland, it releases the emotion of the your thought to the body.

When you work with these exercises, be sure you know what you are asking for. You do not get part of it, you get the whole thing, so think it through.

A positive affirmation is: God is, I am, and We are One. I do not care what you call God. Most people use the term God for want of a better word. Many people call Him Buddha, they call Him Super Intelligence, they call Him the Universal Intelligence, they call Him many things. The important thing is that you call Him.

A very favorable time to impress the subconscious is just before falling asleep. The conscious mind is tired, and it is not going to put up much resistance. In the interim between sleep and wakefulness, you are wide open to suggestion, making it a good time to approach your subconscious.

If you are thinking about making a tape to use before you go to sleep, think through what that tape is saying. Ask yourself why you feel the need to program that kind of thing in you. Be careful how you word it, because if you word it poorly, you can find yourself limited by your own wording. If you do not understand what you are asking for, you can get yourself in trouble. Do not ever let it be a programming based strictly on the ego personality self, but on the greater need within as well. The object of growth is not judgment and punishment, but acceptance.

People sometimes mistakenly believe that by repeating an affirmation they can automatically change their life. This is not always true. An affirmation must be based on logic and reason. Suppose you decide you want to lose thirty pounds. You begin to use an affirmation that says you will lose thirty pounds. In a few days, you find that you have not lost thirty pounds. You are upset and frustrated; the affirmation hasn't worked. What you have done is set up an affirmation that is not logical, so you have defeated its purpose. You are not a stupid person, and you know you cannot lose thirty pounds overnight or in a week.

Perhaps you have to set thirty pounds as the total goal. Change the affirmation to say: At the right and proper rate for me, I lose thirty pounds. I see the result within three months. I suggest you always begin your affirmation with the phrase, "At the right and proper rate or time...." This way you are asking for that which is truly proper for you even if you consciously do not know what is the best way to achieve your goal.

When you wish to make changes in your attitudes, recognize that persistence counts. Trust that it is working and accept that you are changing. Do not stop to test it.

The only way that you can be anything is to live it. You can read all the positive thinking books in the world; but if you do not make one step to live as a positive thinker, you will never become one. Remember also that anybody can backslide along the way. You have to stop and pull the rug out from under yourself every once in a while and say, "Wait a minute, what am I thinking, and what is it doing to me?"

As you work with these methods, do not constantly stop to check that you are achieving your goal. Check instead that you are keeping a positive attitude. If you say, "I believe," you do not have to worry anymore because you *believe*. Affirmations work when you trust and accept what you say. Logic is a rationale based on what you *have known*. Acceptance is based on *faith* that says you can *know more* than what has been known so far.

Do you know what it is to be childlike—not childish, but childlike? Children believe in Santa Clause, the Easter Bunny, elves, and all sorts of wonderful things. They are not afraid because they trust. If every adult would be a little childlike, they would find life much more joyous. Be willing to experience awe, willing to tune into the wonders of the universe both large and small. Logic tells you you will get wet if it rains. Suppose you have an umbrella? If you are going to use logic, you have to use all of it. That might mean raincoats, boots, and umbrellas. You don't have to get wet.

Many people find it very difficult to accept rejection because they want to be in control. They want to know the whats, the whys, and the wherefores. They want to call the shots their way. You can rationalize that something is going to be here, or that this is the thing that is going to make it happen, but that does not mean that is how it is *going* to happen. *The moment you are in is the bridge between what was and what can be*. The moment you are in is where you have to make the decision to accept that rejection does not have to be a painful thing, that rejection can occur for a good reason.

Many of you have been madly in love with someone at a young age and later in life met that same person again. What was your first reaction? Was it, "Oh my, suppose I had married that person—horrors!"? Way back then, it was the greatest thing, but now a new understanding exists. Trust that there is a pattern working beyond your individual personality. Trust that there is an intelligence *within you* that knows more than you think you know. You know by what you have read, seen, and experienced. The superconscious mind of you knows because it came into this world with your total pattern registered in it. Learn to trust it, and it will never fail you.

One of the most difficult rejections to accept is that from family members because the rationale says family units are tight, close, and everybody gets along beautifully. Not necessarily so. Families are human beings with human emotions and human needs. When the children are small, the parents are so willing to love them and give them everything. Later, when they have grown, the parents expect them to take responsibility for their own lives. The *chil - dren* feel rejected. When the children do not oblige, the parents feel rejected. Things happen, but realize that even in a family unit there are some energies that attract and some that repel. You do not have to like your family members, but you do have to love them. You are loving the God in them. The God in you will see the God in them and wish It well. The personality and egos of family members very often will not get along. That does not mean that a vendetta is on. If someone says a few sharp words to you and you spend the next three months planning a family gathering so you can get back at them, you are exercising stupidity, not discernment. You have joined the energy of the insult by accepting it and becoming it. All you have to do is say, "This person needed to unload, but it can only be mine if I accept it as so."

Universal love, loving freely, has nothing to do with personality. It has nothing to do with sex. It has to do with acceptance of your own divinity and of another's unique individuality. You may look at a person as someone whom you do not want to be with, but you must recognize that they too are a divine individual, the soul of which you must love and wish well.

The difference in how an adult and a child approaches life is in their trust factor. The adult mind says, "These are the circumstances, do I trust it? I have to look out for myself, I have to look at all the angles." A child says, "Hello, how are you? You are a nice person." Are you willing to be more open to what can be? If you stop and think, "The moment I am in is a bridge between what has been and what can be," you will realize that how you act at any given moment creates something else. It either brings forth more of the same, or it creates change. Something new being created is usually based on added ingredients, or a change of ingredients. When you are puzzled about trusting, ask yourself what the ingredients are that build a child's trust. Look not only at the ingredients of other people, but also at the ingredients inside yourself. What were the ingredients that built the distrust? What is causing you, at the moment, not to be fully able to trust? What was the interaction that made that distrust?

You cannot approach a new relationship—be it a job, a love relationship, a friendship, whatever—with all the old relationships as your only criteria to what it can be. If the tendency is always to be constantly looking for the old faults in the new thing, then that is what you will manifest. Where your mind is, is where the energy is, and where the energy is, is where the manifestation is.

Universal law says that what you put out comes back to you. Like energy attracts like energy, and that is the thing you have to be aware of. What you give out is like a boomerang. It turns around and comes back. If your trust is based on having a string attached, "I will trust you, if you trust me," it is already in trouble. If you will trust whether another trusts you or not, then that energy of trust in you cannot be tarnished. Learn to trust in the little things, and the growth to trust in the big things will come. Learn to trust that the letter you mailed is going to get there. Learn to trust that when someone says they will call, they will. Take the small issues of trust and make them a part of your life, thus building the ability to trust on a larger scale.The first thing that you have to ask is: Do I trust myself? Do I trust that I am a worthy person? Do I trust that I am able to interact with others? Do I trust that I have what it takes to be a friend? Do not be afraid to trust *you*.

If I could charge everyone in this universe with a lesson, it would be to trust in themselves and to love themselves. If you learn to develop that sense of trust, you will live with such peace of mind that you will come to realize that there is no other way to live. When you learn to believe in yourself, to trust in yourself, and to love yourself, you will not have to worry about anything.

Do you like your job? The people who do not like their job have a string attached to their job. They are expecting that job to act in a certain way, or they cannot accept it as a good job. Granted that you might like to make more money; wanting to progress financially is a part of any job. You have to say to yourself, "If this job is so bad, what am I doing in it? If it is as miserable as I think it is, why am I here? Why have I not done something about it?" In your world, you love to grumble. Use all the energy it takes to grumble to create a step toward change.

This is the new age of spirit and flow. There is nothing that says you cannot change. There is nothing that says there is an age limit to when you can change. You only need to *want* it enough, *believe* in it enough, and trust in it enough to do it. In your present state of mind, you might say that that is a big order; but if you start trusting in the small things, it will lead to being able to trust in the larger things. Start believing you can wear a color you never wore. Start combing your hair differently, or try a different food, because anything that expresses your belief in yourself strengthens your ability to change. As you trust yourself more and more in those areas and permit yourself to make those changes, the ability to change in other things becomes stronger. The realization will then develop that you are no longer rejecting yourself or your potential, and your ability begins to be understood.

When the mind conceives wholeness, wholeness can come. You have to have trust and believe that you can change or stop the rejection process within yourself. Be willing to reject the old ideas and take on the new. There are times when you have to simply accept that what is right and perfect can occur. Be willing to accept *that it is* occurring. If I tell you you are a nice person, do I have to run back every fifteen minutes and tell you again , or can you accept it? If you trust it and believe it, the next time you receive a compliment, it will be easier to trust that too.

There are times when rejection can be a positive force in your life. Rejection is positive when it keeps you from getting into a space that you are not meant to be in. Sometimes what seems to be a painful thing is the greatest thing that ever happened to you. It keeps you from getting into trouble. If you are trusting, you are not going to feel the same about a rejection. You are going to be able to see it as removing you from an unsafe place.

When you feel friction, ask yourself why you feel so threatened. Once you understand where it comes from, you go about turning it around. Let us say you have disagreed with a friend. You send them a note that says, "We don't always see eye to eye, but I want you to know I wish you well." You have then taken care of your end of that friction. There now are two things that can happen. You can have a string attached that says that they are suppose to call you up and tell you it is okay, or write you a lovely note in return. In that case, you have not truly wished them well. You have a preconceived string attached. Now if they do not respond, what happens? *You* have a choice. Do you get mad and start the whole thing all over again, or do you release yourself and let it remain their problem? You have taken care of your end of it; let it go and simply bless them.

In business relationships, there is a natural antagonism which relates to the competitive nature of business. It is necessary to examine the facts of those situations to be sure that your preconceived ideas are correct. Let laughter take the power and pressure away from the situation. Then you can deal with it. You often can become so embroiled in trying to figure things out that you are in a quagmire. The result is that you are losing yourself and losing ground. Stop every once in a while, break the energy, and laugh at it. Come back tomorrow when you have had a chance to rest and pick it up.

Remember this: You are not on this Earth to change

another person. You are on this Earth to change you and nobody else. The only way you can change another person is through changing you. You can never be trusted unless you are trusting. Suppose I were to come into this world to teach, and I said that if everybody doesn't believe everything I say, there is no sense in teaching. How ridiculous! Everybody is going to hear what they want to hear and what they need to hear. They are going to grow with it at the rate they are ready to grow with it. My job is to plant the seeds. What *you* do with it afterwards is going to tell you what kind of crop you are going to have.

> I would like you to ask yourself what it is you feel uneasy about in your life at this moment. Just pick one.
>
> Now ask yourself how important it is on a scale of one to ten.
>
> Now ask what you can do to *alter* it in some way. Don't look to cure it, or end it, but to *alter* it in some way.
>
> What is *your* attitude toward it? How can that be altered in some way?
>
> Now ask yourself when you are going to start to do it. Name a date—any date after today. Plan how you will begin by seeing the small change started by making this decision. Accept that more will follow. Now take a deep breath and declare that *you will begin*.

These steps can help you alter any situation. Altering it in any way creates the ability to really bring change.

You have begun sorting out what you think of as a problem and begun to create a movement within it that can alter it. To change a problem, or a stress factor, let it begin to move. Movement changes the perspective and gives you an opportunity to move out of it. Ask yourself: Why am I antsy? What is bothering me? When you have it pegged, ask: What is *my* part in it? What can *I* do? It does not depend on six other people, what can *I* do?

There is no situation that relates to your life that you do not have a control over, and it starts with your attitude. It starts with your thought patterns and your ability to accept change. You have to be willing to be progressive in thought patterns and thereby change the energy. Institute a movement. Instead of being afraid of something, bless it, surround it with positive attitudes. Those energies will then give you an opportunity to change it. What happens if you meet someone and they look at you blankly? What do you feel inside? What did you do wrong? What is your next thought? Who does that guy think he is? Suppose you smile instead and say hello. A whole different attitude suddenly develops. You are in control. Think the worst and the worst occurs. Think that you can be different, and it will come to be.

Don't put the cart before the horse when planning things. If you are having a party, don't feel that it cannot be successful unless it includes a certain list of specifics.

Instead, ask yourself what the *real* purpose of the affair is. Is it to be with people? Is it to share a camaraderie? If that is the case, then does it really matter whether it is filet mignon or peanut butter? If the real purpose is friendship, why are you letting all these other things get in the way? Do not put the power in the material things, but in the essence of the purpose of it. You will find it more fun.

There are no wrong decisions. It is what you do with it that makes the difference. Remember once you have made a decision, put all your energy into that decision. Do not put your energy into looking back. See your position in relationship to the situation in a different way. As soon as you do that, you will feel different. The old criteria has to fall for the new to come.

Try using these steps to understand rejection:

Think of the last time you felt rejected and ask yourself the following questions:
1. What were you expecting from it?
2. What had you put into it? What were your attitudes?
3. How much of you were you willing to change to meet it half way?
4. How much were you wrapped in your own preconceived ideas that you could not see the need of the other person or the other factors in the situation?
5. Were you trying to interact in the situation solely for your own good? Were you willing to learn from it?
6. What difference does it make?
7. Where do I go from here?

Keep this in mind: Reruns do not make changes. Did you ever notice that after you look at a television program reruns fifteen times, they are not funny anymore, they are not tragic anymore, they are not anything anymore? They are just old records being played. That is what you do when you enter a new phase and try to rerun the old program. All it does is become very dull after a while. It is like running in place, you do not move forward.

The following affirmation will assist you in accepting your own positive strengths. Take a deep breath and repeat:

I am a divine child of God with divine rights of my own and I shall be fulfilled.

I accept the power within to change that which leads me astray. From within myself, I draw the strength, the realization, and the joy of changing my life.

I can and I will, by acceptance and release, be whole. Through the acceptance of the power within me, through release of old patterns, comes the won derful realization that I am truly in control. I am divine power in perfect action.

Think of the times you have had a problem. When you looked at it a few days later, you wondered why you were so upset. In the initial moment, you got swallowed by the emotion.

Rejection is a normal phase of interchange. Do not see

it as something you must accept, but rather as an expression of emotional needs. The power to give and take rejection rests within each individual. Take a close look at what occurs, gain from it, and move on.

Fear is not an entity in itself, but rather a pattern of behavior. The antedote to fear lies in shedding light on the unknown.

CHAPTER VI

SEX AND SENSUALITY

One of the most important factors to remember when you are dealing with the subject of sex and the sensual element of the self in relationship to spiritual growth is that you cannot separate the mind, the body, and the spirit. Your mind interprets your feelings. Those feelings affect the body. A deep spiritual understanding helps to keep the mind and body in balance. All that you think registers deep within you in the subconscious mind. You register your feelings as well. Therefore, even though you may close your conscious mind to a situation, your subconscious will still be releasing the feelings and emotions within it.

Whatever happens within you is sensed and reacted to in all of you. As you become more aware spiritually, that spirituality is expressed and interpreted by each part of you. The physical body interprets the awakening sensuality as sex. The sensuality and awareness of the mind and spirit is very different from sex. Sensuality permits you to be aware through your senses. Sexuality deals with body chemistry. The mind enhances or decreases the effect.

As you grow spiritually, you begin to reach out to others. You begin to want to know, experience, and understand as well as help others. You reach out spiritually and physically when you embrace another. You do not think of that embrace as a sexual thing; you think of it as an expanded awareness toward another. What happens if that embrace goes beyond a momentary thing? When that embrace is held longer than the momentary hello, it is awakening every other sense in the body. The sensual self begins to respond to the body chemistry of the self, and sometimes that which starts off as a spiritual thing can get out of hand.

The rationale is: If you love one another unconditionally in mind, body, and spirit, what difference does it make? It makes a difference in this respect: A loving embrace that says "I care" is one thing, but if that embrace goes beyond that, it takes on additional responsibilities. If your embrace gives the message that it is more than the spiritual hello, you have the responsibility of that. You have the responsibility of your interpretation of it as well as the other party's.

Your culture has let sex become a bit of a god. Everyone worships sex. If you think of every commercial that sells a product in your world today, ninety-five percent of them deal with sensuous areas and attitudes. They deal with promises implied and unseen, and very soon you begin to think that is reality. You are a body with a chemistry of its own. Your body chemistry reacts in a variety of ways. It

150

can be strongly attracted to one personality while being repelled by another. Energy, body chemistry, and mental attitudes all affect the developmental potential of these relationships.

If you have a sense that the only thing that can make you a whole person is to have a sexual partner, or a sexual relationship, what happens to all the other parts of you? What do you do when you are not consumed in the sexual aspect of your involvement? You cannot be in a sensual, sexual being twenty-four hours a day. You might initially try, but it will get a bit tiring. The point is that *all of you* reacts to everything *you* do.

Think for a minute about what happens when you look at pornographic pictures or read sexy novels. Have you noticed that one writer can give you a suggestion, and you can imagine the whole scene; and another one has to give it to you play-by-play? In most cases, the better writer is the one who lets you use your imagination. It is much more creative. When you are presented with sexually stimulating material, the mind creates visual images that then creates *sensual attitudes* and *sexual reactions*. When you are provoked by sexually stimulating material, *the whole of your - self* comes into action through the sensual stimulation, and it is here your free will decides how far this fantasy will go.

Anyone can read a passage in a book that is very racy. However, if they forget to read the rest of the book and read nothing but that passage for the rest of the week, they are out of balance. If, however, they see that particular passage within the context of the rest of the book, they see it as part of life as depicted in that particular situation, and it is kept in its proper place.

In your culture today, the attitude of sex and sensuality has taken such a prominent place that it is out of balance. People are not seeing themselves as happy beings unless they are able to say they are sexually involved. This is just as unbalanced as the time when nobody talked about it. Sex is. Sensuality can be. Love is.

The degree that you take it to and the attitude that you approach it with gives it the quality that will manifest. The quality of a love is based on each individual's understanding of what they think love is. One person might say, "She (loves me very much because she does everything I want, but she doesn't understand me." or, "He loves me very much because he gives me everything I want, but he doesn't hear me when I speak."

The interpretation you have individually or collectively when approaching love, sex, and sensuality creates the type of exchange it is. The love you have for a child, for a spouse, for a lover, or for your pet is different; but it still affects the whole being. You have to permit yourself to recognize that if you are having reactions within the body, there are thought processes going on in the mind.

If you are becoming more aware of everything around you, you are becoming aware also of what is going on in those around you. If you are feeling sensuous about yourself, then you can begin to feel sensual about another. You are, therefore, breaking down barriers and walls that were once there. Where you place the thought pattern determines what is going to happen with that awareness.

You have a body and you have body chemistry. To have sexual desires when the right body chemistry is created is normal. Sexual desire is not abnormal and need not be frowned upon. If you are using your body sensuously, use it in its *high* potential, not in its low force. Let your sex be a mystical experience. Let it be a loving and beautiful thing, not something animalistic. Know that to love someone and to become involved with someone is to do so on *all* levels. Sex is only one aspect of a love relationship, but often it seems it is the only aspect that many spend much effort on. Know that you are meant to express your sexuality and to experience sensual expression, but that should be done from the high part of yourself and not be something that is entered into casually or with little regard. To have a relationship that is real and lasting, their needs to be mental and spiritual union as well.

When you become involved with another on a sensual level, you have a choice to make. It can be a one-night stand or part of a relationship which encompasses the whole of that person. Your evolution requires you to use your sexual expression in concert with all the other aspects of your personality and expects that you take *full* responsibility for all that you commit yourself to. It is not something that should be entered into lightly.

Body chemistry is spontaneous. What happens with it will be based on your mental attitude. Mind will decide whether to accept or whether body chemistry should take a "cold shower." It is a very practical interplay between the mind, which has the final say in all matters, and the body. When the mind takes over, it decides when it is appropriate to respond and when it is not.

When love exists in a caring form, sex is a mystical union. When that does not exist, it is a mechanical act. It is then a body-chemistry release. If that is the only kind of sex you experience, you will never feel fulfilled. You will need more and more because all of you is not a part of the experience. You have only the body chemistry responding. Sex is the joining of two beings. You can come together and fight, or you can come together and love. You can come together in sex in the same way. It can either be a bestial thing or a beautiful thing. How you are thinking and feeling about it makes the difference. Fulfillment can only come from complete involvement *in a responsible manner.*

To be a sensual being, there is a balance needed. To be sensual is to be aware of *your* being, but it does not mean being in love with your body. It means being aware of it, being happy with it, and being comfortable with it. There is a fine line that is drawn. Who draws the line? You do. You know when you are permitting the sensory factors to take over with little concern for the rest of you. The one thing that you must realize is that *you* control it.

It is possible to have sensual sensations during a meditative process as the body becomes aware of itself. You feel wrapped in a loving energy that is peaceful but, at the same time, are really feeling yourself sensually. This has nothing to do with physical sex. Man often translates this feeling as sexual. How you have thought about yourself and your body enters into how you interpret the feeling. You can express it and accept it as a high or low experience.

The body is the temple of the soul. It is where the *real you* lives. Just as you would want to have a clean and well cared for home for the body to live in, you want a clean and well cared for home for the soul to live in. If you begin to think in those terms, you begin to respect the body. As you begin to respect your body, you truly begin to love it. Loving it, again, is not on the S-E-X level. It is on the combined level of mind, body, and spirit.

A question: Do you like your body? It is yours. It is special. It talks to you. If you encourage it, it reacts to you. If you ignore it, you are never going to feel together. It is important to know that loving yourself—mind, body, and spirit—is the most important thing you can do.

Look at your body with the true understanding of what it was created for. Looking at the body with a true understanding of its beauty has nothing to do with style, fashion, or weight. Your body is the temple of the soul, and that is very, very important. It should be loved, and you should not be afraid to touch it and say, "Good morning, I love you." If you are treating your body as if it were the scum of the Earth, it will react to you in that manner.

Just as the sensual self lets you understand the body, you must also let that sensual self permit you to understand the thought patterns that control the body. Suppose I said to you, "Sit up straight! Pull in your stomach!" These are thought suggestions, but if you hear them, the natural instinct is to follow them. If you think such thoughts, your body will accept them. You have the ability to control where you take your body with your mind. You will bring to it the amount of respect you want it to have. To understand the body, you have to understand the inner you.

Just for one minute, look at your hand. Just look at your hand and tell it you love it. Look at it and think of what it does for you in the course of one day. If you want to caress someone, you need that hand. That hand is serving. Why should it not be loved? There is often fear of loving the body because it is thought of as sexual. The body, the magnificent machine that is serving you throughout your life, deserves respect and love.

Put your arms around yourself and, for one minute, think about what a great person you are. You may be embarrassed. You should not be because you *are* a wonderful person. Think of all the times you have held hands with someone. How can you not respect the hand and love the hand that permitted that to happen? Let us move to the elbow. How could you ever lean on anything if you did not have an elbow? How could you ever give someone the "wake up?" If you take your body one part at a time and see its service to you, you will begin to like it more. Put it all together, and you will see the beautiful gift it is.

When you succeed in developing a relationship with another person based on *all aspects* of the self, you have taken the energy away from physical focus alone. It is a mystical union when it is in the high force of love. In this high force, the love or the sex exchanged is of a much higher energy, and it yields a sustained warmth which truly satisfies the need within man for the answering of his sensual self.

There is a great confusion in your world over which emotional responses are correct and which ones are not. A good deal of energy is used worrying whether lust is helping to destroy you. Remember, every single one of your emotions are there for a reason—even lust. They are legal for thirty seconds. After that, they are an ego trip. The point is this: Body chemistry is spontaneous. You label it lust. You say you lust after someone, and then the mind takes over. Now you must question the feasibility of the body's reaction. It is a free will choice. You make the decision. *What goes with the decision is the responsibility for it.*

There are times when you have very intimate moments with your spouse or lover. There are times when your eyes meet across the room, and this is equally as intimate an exchange but you are not even touching. When you are apart from each other, you do not see each other at all, but the mind can bring that loving look, or loving feeling, to life within you. Again, you will feel that sensual, loving feeling. It has nothing to do with body against body. That is but one fragment of it. It is, when properly developed, so much more than that. When you think back to all the loving times, do not be afraid to relive all the sensual qualities of those times.

In every Age, there have been different attitudes created about sex. They are created by the culture. You are experiencing many changes in how your society thinks about sex. Many aspects of sex and sensual attitudes are today very different from even a few years ago. With these changes come conflicts for some who were raised in a period with a particular point of view toward sex, when they confront some of the newer attitudes. Remember, the only thing that is constant in this new Age is change; and just as there have been many changes in recent years toward sexual attitudes, know that there will continue to be changes coming forth in the culture toward this subject. However, no matter how much the attitudes may change, the fact remains the same. Love is mind, body, and spirit in perfect accord with another being. *Love* is never sex alone.

In your culture today, there are some frightening consequences from misuse of the sexual energies. There are many suffering from the devastating disease known as AIDS. As I have said before, there are no half packages. If you run the road, you get the view. If you have an abundance of sexual relationships that are not based on knowing the individual, on knowing the quality of what is happening, then you take the risk of those things. When there is an abundance of that kind of an expression, there is an abundance of all the things that go with it.

When man first came to the Earth—the essence of

man—there was an androgynous body of light that was both male and female that procreated from within the self. At that point, man did not have to merge with another. As the denseness began to occur, as the vibration lowered, the more animalistic senses in relation to the physical density began. Gradually there developed a leaning toward the senses, rather than the spirit, and the androgynous body split. Within each half of that androgynous being is both male and female energy. Everyone is both. In each particular lifetime, there is a leaning toward one, but you must also permit the other to flow. The female must understand the masculine strength of herself, and the male must understand his gentler feminine side. Remember, you are working back to the androgynous form again.

If you are going to know yourself and become aware, you are going to have to let that awareness bring you to the highest point of your sensuality and your sexuality. This means sex and your sensual expression is not a bestial thing, but something that deserves respect, honor, acceptance, and love. As long as those ingredients are there, you are making the decision about your sensuality based on the correct criteria, and that is what is important.

There is the notion that karma has a lot to do with sex. It is used as a mighty excuse in your world. There are many people claiming karmic attachment as an excuse for an affair they simply *had* to have. Karma has become a word bandied about which is very much misunderstood in your world. It has become an excuse. If you are bringing forward a karmic pattern with someone, you will have emotional memories of it, but that does not necessarily mean that the same thing is supposed to happen in this life. You may have to meet that person and overcome those feelings. You might like this person and have them as one of your best friends in this life, but it does not have to be a repeat performance of what it was before.

I constantly see people in your world who are frustrated and confused within themselves. Because of many attitudes that are popular in the culture, they feel as if they should always be sexually involved. Other times they feel as if this may not be the right path. Within them is a genuine sense of confusion and uncertainty. You need to sit down and have a talk with *you* and ask yourself: What am I doing? Why am I looking for what I think I'm supposed to be looking for when I don't know if I really want to look for it? It is like saying everybody has to ice skate. Some people do not have strong ankles. Some people do not like the cold. You have to permit yourself to determine what *you* want in your life and know that when you determine it, *you accept the responsibility of it*. The two can never be separated. Every action has a reaction, and the only place your action comes back is to you.

A person develops individually. Throughout life, they will encounter many with whom they will have close associations. In the early school years, a child will form many enduring relationships. As the child moves through the years, some of those friendships will fall by the wayside. As this child becomes a young adult and enters college, new friendships will form. Here, again, as the student develops into a young adult, many of those college era friendships will fall to be replaced by new associations formed in adulthood. Nothing in any of the previous friendships that waned is bad, it is only that the needs and the focus of the individual have changed.

People need change. Some friendships will alter, but there will be enough that remains to share between them that the friendship itself continues. People will change and will literally outgrow each other. They will separate and leave that association. It will not be a bitter parting because it has come from a transition within them to something else. What was a great love affair might become a good friendship. Others, who do not understand the changes because they do not understand themselves, will create angers and resentments, which then make the separation painful. In time, the pain is healed; and it is usually healed by a new comprehension, a new understanding, and new growth.

In a world that is in constant change, the energies will affect each person differently. There was a time when two people came together and would be together for all of their lives. As the world has become smaller and change has become more prevalent, the energies seem to have a different effect. There was a time when a child grew up in one town or area. Everything in that area was his. It was his school, his library, his this, his that; and he had a great pride and association with it. He probably married in that same town and raised children in that same town. In today's world, a child will have lived in six, eight, or ten different places by the time he reaches an age of having a serious thought of relationships. Therefore, his attitude about what stability and a steady foundation is will be different.

Celibacy is a free will choice, but to be celibate does not necessarily mean that you are a higher or more spiritual being. The person who handles correctly the emotions in his live and who handles himself with dignity and respect in relationship to sex is equally as developed. Celibacy has long been part of the disciplines of various teachings. By removing the energy from the sacral chakra, the inclination to sex is diminished. You have one energy. Where you direct it and the level in which it is functioning controls the outcome. Celibacy takes the mind away from the body chemistry and lets the mind bring the energy to higher levels. Understand that the mind can bring that energy to the sacral chakra and function within that chakra in an equally divine manner. The energy can move from one area to another as directed by your mind. A person who chooses to be celibate must choose it because that is what he wants.

You may choose to be celibate; and if you have truly chosen it in yourself, you will not be miserable. If you have accepted it because you have been told you must, you will not be comfortable with it. Any decision about you has to come from your own inner divine guidance. You decide. When you decide, you live with it; and you live with it in peace. That is what is important.

Sensual attitudes are born with you. You relate to them all through life on different levels of understanding. In early life, you learn about your own body in preparation for

greater understanding later. Children are not afraid of their
bodies. They will go through periods when they are very
enamored with them. They touch and feel their bodies, and
adults will become horrified. Everything a child learns is
from touching, tasting, smelling, seeing, or hearing. Watch
a child. He will pick something up, shake it, rattle it, or
smell it. When he comes to know about his body, he is
going to touch it, he is going to want to smell it, and he is
going to want to know what is going on with it. It is a normal curiosity. He is awakening his senses and learning
about them. It should not be something that disturbs you,
but at the same time, he needs to be taught that his body is
special. The body is private, the body is special, but that
does not mean you make it a hidden thing. When children
ask a question about sex, they should be answered, but not
inundated. You give them what the question calls for.
Inquire about what it is they really need to know and then
explain it.

Some children are quite aggressive during the adoles-
cent phase of their development. They want to have
answers to everything. They often want to know more
about, not only their body, but the bodies of others as well.
A precocious child needs to be told their body is special and
private. You permit them to hug you, but you do not permit
them to touch you with undue familiarity. Let them begin to
learn the difference between doing what they please,
because they feel or want to, and understanding that there
are times when they cannot do that. Do not make it a thing
that implies it is naughty. Say, "That's okay, just remember
this is my body, and I take care of who touches it."

A matter of great concern in your culture now is contraception. In earlier times, procreation was very necessary; but just as things change in all areas, there are times when procreation can become a danger. To bear a child is a free will decision. It is usually made before you enter this world; but because of free will, you must re-evaluate your decision once you are in this world. You might have programmed two or three children before entering, but once you are here, you might decide that one is enough because you have to feed it, clothe it, and so forth. Any decision made in relationship to this deals with your free will and what you are comfortable with. In the first months of a child's development, it is a biological outgrowth of the mother and father. When the mother feels life, the soul has entered. At that point, it is a being that you are carrying.

Because everybody says sex is great and everybody's doing it does not mean that you have to. You were given free will. You were given a mind, a body, and a spirit. Let yourself be guided by that inner light which will take you through sexual experiences physically, mentally, and spiritually in perfect harmony. Remember, if you let others talk you into something you are not ready for, it is you who will carry the guilt trips, disease, nervous reactions, and fear.

What is erroneous in your culture today is the use of abortion as birth control. There are many other methods of birth control in your world. You should not have to go through conception and then an act of self-mutilation when there are other methods of avoiding pregnancy. When individuals have an abortion—for whatever reason— it is important to understand that it happened in that point in time. They must not anchor themselves to it for the rest of their lives. They must go on with life and go on living and, perhaps, bear a child at another time if it is right and proper for them. They cannot sit in judgement of themselves for something that occurred at one point in time in their lives. If they sit in judgement of that one point in their past, it can very well destroy the whole life. They must learn from the experience, accept the responsibility for their choice, and move on.

In many instances, there are complications that surround the decision to have an abortion. For example, if a woman who is mentally incapable becomes pregnant through rape, others around the woman may decide that an abortion is the best thing for her. In situations like these, the person who bears the responsibility for these decisions and who has a karmic debt depends on the situation. You have no way of knowing why that child is there, or why it is taken away.

Masturbation is the body's response to a stimulus. The body chemistry reacts, and it reacts very often to something seen, something read, or something heard about. The body chemistry reacts and needs to feel the fulfillment that it is experiencing through the senses. The masturbation becomes the mechanical physical act that makes it happen. If you spend all your time in masturbation, it is out of balance. Anything that becomes a total absorption becomes imbalance.

When two people have lived together for a number of

years, there often develops between them a lessening of the feeling of desire or attraction. There are many reasons why this may happen. First of all, understand that when we talk about sexual energy, we are talking about a body and about things that a body has in it. Realize that how that body is fed can affect its ability to be sensual. Look for the cause. It can be that they are becoming disenchanted of the other person's attitudes and are not feeling in synchronization with them. If communication is lessening, people will drift apart. To reinstitute verbal exchange between them can often reverse the situation. It can be a process of aging. It can be nutrients that are needed in the body, and it can be the recognition that there is more to their union than sex. Two people who no longer feel the physical excitement for each other may be perfectly comfortable and happy on mental and spiritual levels. For them, holding hands is their sex.

If a relationship is based on sharing the whole being, the lessening of sex will not be a terrifying thing. It can be the most rewarding time of the whole relationship if they accept that sex is only one part of their relationship. A true relationship is based on mental, emotional, and spiritual exchange as well as sex.

There are times when two souls agree to become associated before they enter this world. This is true in some instances, but not all. Just as a woman may determine that she would like to bear children and that perhaps she would like to have a large or a small family, once she is in the physical body in this world she has the divine right of free

will and may re-evaluate that. It looks very easy from my
world. Remember , while you are in the spirit world, many
arrangements or decisions my be made, but once you are in
the physical body, you possess free will over what you
choose to do. It may be that a prearranged marriage
between two souls will instead be a friendship. It does not
have to be what was previously agreed upon.

The demeaning of sex and the belief that sex is dirty
came from cultural teachings over the years. Love is love. It
is felt and expressed in many ways. He who stands in judgment of another will stand judged. It does not matter what
kind of love is being expressed, it matters that *love* is being
expressed. If it is a bisexual, homosexual—whatever—it
can still be a beautiful thing or a bestial thing. The quality
of the thought and the attitude brought to it is what makes
the difference. *This does not mean that you are removed
from the responsibility of your relationship.* It must be
understood that any expression of love has a responsibility
that accompanies it. There are no half packages. He who
cheats is cheated.

You are coming into an era where things are in the open
rather than hidden. The important realization must be that it
is a free will choice *with the responsibilities of that choice.*
Each individual is responsible for himself. What I am saying to you is that so much concern is given to other people's
sexual attitudes when the only attitude of sex that you have
the right to have is your own. What are you doing with
your sexual self? What are you doing with *your* attitudes
about sex? How are *you* handling you?

Sex is, and it is going to be as long as humanity exists. If it were not for sex, you would not be. Somebody created you. The genetic aspect of yourself is created *to house a soul*. If that is the purpose of sex, you may ask how sex can be wrong. What can be wrong is *how* you manifest sex. As you enter sex and permit the body chemistry to flow, what you think and feel about it has a lot to do with what results. That is what makes the difference. You can take it to a low place or a high place. You control it.

Because sex has been given such a place of prominence in your world, it has begun to be seen as the criteria for being a success. There is a tremendous emotional attachment to sex which often leads to associations based more on body chemistry than what is truly the best. Because people believe that sex indicates their success as a person, they often enter a relationship rather than say no. The most important thing to remember is that unless a relationship is entered with a strong sense of it being right for you, it cannot fulfill you. Sex because "everyone is doing it" is no reason for sex. If you feel insecure by making a decision *not* to enter sex, find out why. The answer will be your fulfillment.

In today's culture, you are exposed to sexuality in many ways. Often this can prove to be frustrating. You have to make your inner space a place you can go to be away from that which you feel is inundating you. You have the divine right to refuse any energy that is around you. It does not mean you refuse another person's right to it, but you don't accept it as yours.

If you are in a relationship and become miffed about something, you will bring that attitude into your next sexual encounter. You, in that moment, are directing your attitude to that relationship. You can hurt it, or you can help it, but *you* are doing something to it. If you are hurting that relationship, that may be an indication that you are not truly happy in that association. Maybe you need to examine yourself to find out if that relationship is really fulfilling you. If you are going into something with an attitude that is not positive, you should not be in it in the first place. If it is going to work for you, it must be positive.

Did you ever notice that when you learn to drive a car, at first you are awkward at it? You have to think of all of it as separate parts—this is the brake, this is the clutch, this is the gear shift, and this is the speedometer. After you have learned to drive, you do not think of those as separate parts. You get in the car knowing you can drive and you drive. When you become more aware of yourself, you have control, you get in *you*, and you drive. You do not have to worry about whether it is your sexual you, your thinking you, your body, or your spirit. You are in synchronization.

If you keep in mind that your thought patterns create your reality, you will understand why you must understand why you feel the way you do about sex. Remember also that as you change your thought patterns, you change your attitudes. Sex in itself cannot create happiness, only the merger of the whole being—mind, body, and spirit—can bring fulfillment.

Some people spend so much time focusing on themselves that they make the body a god. I am not talking about exercise, lifting weights, or whatever you want to do for physical prowess. That is not what we are talking about. If you spend more time looking at your body in the mirror than you do using it to make your life work, you are out of balance. If you think that your body is the only thing that creates your image, you are not in touch with all of you. You are a triad of mind, body, and spirit; and they must be permitted to interact. Your mind is the director of the energy within the body. Your thoughts become your feelings.

You are unique. You are an energy package that no one else can be. That is a wonderful thing. Permit yourself to appreciate that and use that uniqueness to gain what you want in life. The key is to think before you act and not to let anything or anyone make you feel less than you are. In other words, love and respect yourself enough to use your potential fully—mind, body, and spirit.

CHAPTER VII

CLOSING COMMENTS

Through everything you have read in this book, you have come to the realization that the key is yourself, that how you think and act and interact creates the atmosphere around you, the community around you, and virtually your universe. Recognize that you are an expression of polarity, therefore, you will seek balance throughout your evolutionary path. The desire to change comes from evolution in process, not from something being wrong with you. That which you felt was perfect at any given point in your life, might, five or six years later, need change. By the very nature of the changing energies in your universe itself, man is urged to experience and grow.

In working with the recognition of your uniqueness and the realization of your part in the creation of your life, it is most important to understand that *you are not on trial dur - ing the search*. You are coming into a wiser, more evolved recognition of the self, a self that does not need the same support systems from others that it did during the Piscean Age. Realize that evolution means progression. It means strength and a movement to a higher space. The moment one stops blaming everyone else in the world, they recognize the power they have. This does not mean that something someone says will not cause you to feel wounded; it does not mean that circumstances do not occur outside yourself that make you feel invalidated; but it is at that moment that the full realization of the power of the self must be recognized.

Recognize that to be put down does not mean that you *are* down. Recognize that no matter what happens outside yourself, the degree of pain created is by *your* reaction to it, not by the incident itself. When something supposedly goes wrong in life, recognize that that is the way it is. Move into a new perspective that is not based on what you had expected of it, but based on your realization of your ability to make something better out of it

When children are learning to walk, they fall down a lot. When people are trying to get a new focus on life, they take several steps forward and sometimes one backward. Why do they step back? To get a stronger foothold. Take the perspective that when something happens that does not move the way you think it is supposed to, *that* is your step back to get a better foothold. It is then that you take a new look at what, perhaps, was *meant* to be versus what you *expected* to be. In every incident, you begin to recognize that you are in control and that the only thing that takes you out of control is for you not to recognize change as growth and movement to a higher space.

You were born unique, but uniqueness in itself grows. Look at yourself in the full recognition that through the varying changes, through the polarity of sometimes having things good and sometimes not so good, you have grown to the unique and wonderful being you are now. I want you to recognize fully that no matter how much change you think you need, you are unique in the divine energy of creative force *right now*. Remember that, my friend, and know that each time you take new perspective, you open a whole new avenue of evolution, growth, and wonderment for yourself. So be it.

Decision making is based on what is available and the expectation of the choice maker.

Personal Notes

Personal Progress Observations

JULIAN TAPES AVAILABLE

Over the years, Julian has taught over 150 classes on many subjects. Tapes of his teachings are available. If you would like to receive a tape list, please mail your request to:

Rev. June K. Burke Enterprises
101 Arthursburg Road
LaGrangeville, NY 12540-5933